The Practical Guide on How to Talk to Anyone

65 Simple Secrets to Confident Small Talk, Effective Communication, Building Lasting Relationships, and Accelerating Career Success

Parker Lawson

Contents

Your Free Gift

As a thank you for your purchase, I'm offering my readers two bonus eBooks.

Simply visit the link below to enjoy instant access!

https://parkerlawsonbooks.com/Free-Gift

Book 1 *"Unlock Your Emotional Intelligence: 10 Daily Habits to Improve Social Connections"*

Inside the book, you will discover:

✔ Daily habits to enhance emotional awareness and build stronger connections.

✔ Simple techniques to master empathy, active listening, and self-awareness.

✔ Effective strategies to reframe negative thoughts and develop a more positive mindset.

✔ And so much more!

This book as a quick guide to check and improve your emotional intelligence in daily life. Make sure to grab the free book today!

Book 2 *"How to Stop Overthinking Everything: 7 Simple Strategies to Emotional Clarity, Self-Trust, and Inner Calm"*

Inside the book, you will discover strategies on how to:

✔ Pause spiraling thoughts before they take over.

✔ Feel your emotions instead of overanalyzing them.

✔ Release the need for certainty and control.

✔ Talk to yourself with compassion instead of criticism.

✔ Build self-trust, one decision at a time.

✔ And so much more!

This book is your invitation to ground yourself in the present moment and create emotional safety from the inside out. You don't need to battle your thoughts. You just need to understand them. Let's grab the free book today!

Introduction

I remember standing at the edge of a crowded conference room, my heart racing as I clutched my coffee cup like a lifeline. The room buzzed with animated conversations, but I felt frozen, trapped in a familiar loop of self-doubt. *Should I approach that group by the window? What if I say something awkward? What if they're already deep in conversation and don't want to be interrupted?*

If you have ever felt that knot in your stomach before walking into a networking event or found yourself scrolling through your phone to avoid making eye contact in a room full of strangers, know that you are not alone. We are living in what I call the "connection paradox." In an era of unprecedented digital connectivity, genuine human connection often feels more elusive than ever.

The irony of our modern world is not lost on me. We can instantly message someone on the other side of the planet, yet many of us struggle to strike up a conversation with the person sitting next to us at a coffee shop. We have hundreds, sometimes thousands, of social media connections but fewer deep, meaningful relationships than previous generations. We are constantly "connected" through our devices, yet studies show that loneliness and social isolation are reaching epidemic levels.

But here's what gives me hope and drives me to share these insights with you: The ability to connect meaningfully with others isn't a magical trait bestowed upon a lucky few at birth. It is a skill—one that can be learned, practiced, and mastered. The same person who once hid behind their coffee cup can become someone who confidently walks into any room, initiates engaging conversations, and builds lasting relationships.

I know because I have lived through this transformation. As a conference speaker and educator now, people often assume I have always been naturally outgoing. They would be surprised to know about the time I literally hid in a bathroom stall during a professional mixer or how I once stumbled through an important presentation so badly that I seriously considered changing careers. These are not just embarrassing stories I share for entertainment—they are pivotal moments that drove me to understand the science and art of human connection.

That bathroom stall incident? It became the catalyst for my research into social anxiety and how our minds process unfamiliar social situations. The failed presentation? It led me to study how master communicators structure their messages and connect with audiences. Each uncomfortable moment, each missed opportunity for connection, pushed me to dig deeper into understanding how genuine human connections are formed and maintained.

Through extensive research, training, and countless conversations with people from all walks of life, I have discovered something remarkable: There is a pattern to meaningful connection. Better yet, this pattern can be broken down into practical, actionable steps that anyone can learn. The 65 secrets I share in this book are not theoretical concepts pulled from academic papers (though they are backed by solid research). They are real-world strategies tested in the laboratory of daily life—in boardrooms and birthday parties, in job interviews and first dates, in quiet coffee shops and bustling networking events.

What makes this book different is its focus on practical application. While understanding the psychology of connection is valuable, knowing exactly what to say when someone asks, "So, what do you do?" is invaluable. Each chapter combines scientific insights with specific scripts, scenarios, and step-by-step guidance you can implement immediately. You'll learn not just the why but the how of effective communication.

I've seen these principles transform the lives of countless individuals. There was Sarah, a brilliant engineer who was repeatedly passed over for promotion despite her technical expertise—until she learned how to communicate her ideas effectively to non-technical stakeholders. Now, she leads her department's largest innovation initiatives. Or Marcus, who spent years feeling like an outsider at industry events until he mastered the art of authentic networking. Today, he has built a thriving consultancy based largely on relationships formed at those same events he used to dread.

These transformations did not happen overnight and did not require these individuals to become different people. Instead, they learned to harness their authentic selves while developing the skills to connect meaningfully with others. They discovered that effective communication is not about becoming more extroverted or mastering manipulation tactics—it is about learning to express your true self in ways that resonate with others.

This book is for you if you have ever felt your heart race before walking into a room full of strangers, if you want to move beyond surface-level small talk to build genuine connections, or if you are tired of feeling overlooked in professional settings. It is for those who find themselves running out of things to say in conversations, want to transform casual acquaintances into meaningful relationships, or long to strengthen bonds with family and friends, even when conflicts arise.

It is for anyone who wishes to maintain authentic connections with loved ones through life's ups and downs, who wants to navigate disagreements while preserving relationships, and who's ready to stop watching life happen from the sidelines and start actively participating in it. Most importantly, it is for anyone who believes, as I do, that meaningful connection is not just a nice-to-have but a fundamental human need—one that we all deserve to fulfill.

The journey we are about to embark on is not about becoming someone else—it is about becoming more fully yourself while learning to connect authentically with others. It is about trans-forming those awkward silences into meaningful exchanges, those nervous butterflies into excitement, and those missed opportunities into moments of connection.

As we dive into these 65 secrets, remember that mastering communication is not about perfection—it is about progress. You don't need to implement every strategy at once. Start with what resonates most strongly with you. Practice in low-stakes situations. Celebrate small wins. Most importantly, be patient with yourself as you develop these new skills.

In the chapters ahead, we will explore everything from the science of first impressions to the art of deep listening, from handling difficult conversations to leaving lasting positive impressions. Each secret builds upon the others, creating a comprehensive toolkit for confident, effective communication in any situation.

Are you ready to step out from behind that coffee cup? To transform your professional relationships? To deepen your personal connections? To become someone who can genuinely talk to anyone?

Turn the page, and let's begin this journey together. Your next meaningful conversation is closer than you think.

Chapter 1
The Foundations of Great Communication

P icture this: I am at a conference in San Francisco, observing two colleagues in what appears to be the most natural conversation I have ever witnessed. Maria, a senior executive, is speaking with James, a new hire, about their shared passion for urban gardening. Their interaction flows effortlessly: Maria leans in slightly as James describes his rooftop tomato plants, her face lighting up with genuine interest. When she responds, she references specific details from his story, building upon them with her own experiences. James's initial nervousness melts away as he realizes he's truly being heard, not just politely tolerated.

Understanding the Basics of Talking

The basics of talking might seem, well, basic. But here is the truth I have discovered through years of research and observation: Most of us think we are better communicators than we actually are. We assume that because we can speak, we know how to truly connect. This section will challenge that assumption and provide you with concrete tools to transform your everyday interactions.

Secret #1: The Power of Active Listening

During a particularly challenging workshop I was leading, an executive named Thomas approached me during the break, his expression a mixture of revelation and regret. "I have been doing it wrong for twenty years," he said, shaking his head. "I thought I was a great listener because I could remember and repeat everything people said. But today, I realized I was just waiting for my turn to speak."

Thomas's story is not unique. Research shows that when someone feels truly heard, something remarkable happens in their brain (Aknin et al., 2020). The experience activates the same neural reward centers as receiving physical gifts or monetary rewards. In other words, giving someone your full attention is literally as valuable as giving them a present.

When it comes to focusing fully on the speaker, creating the right environment is crucial. Physical positioning plays a vital role in demonstrating attention. Beyond just facing the speaker, consider the subtle messages your posture sends. A slight forward lean shows engagement without invading personal space. Your shoulders should be relaxed, creating an open, receptive stance that invites sharing.

In busy environments, strategic positioning becomes even more critical. Find spaces where background activity won't compete for attention. If you are in an office, consider positioning yourself so that doorways or high-traffic areas aren't in your conversation partner's line of sight. These minor environmental adjustments can significantly impact the quality of your interaction.

The art of paraphrasing requires a delicate balance. When reflecting someone's words back to them, the goal isn't to simply repeat what they've said but to demonstrate understanding of both content and emotion. For example, instead of just saying, "So, you're frustrated with the project timeline," you might say, "I hear how the delayed timeline is affecting both your team's morale and your ability to meet client commitments." This deeper reflection shows you are grasping both the practical and emotional implications of their situation.

Thoughtful follow-up questions serve as bridges to deeper understanding. Rather than asking generic questions, develop the skill of crafting questions that emerge naturally from what you are hearing. When someone shares a challenge they're facing, asking, "What led you to that conclusion?" opens the door to understanding their thought process and experiences. "How did that impact your approach going forward?" invites reflection on both consequences and adaptations.

Secret #2: Nonverbal Communication Speaks Louder Than Words

The impact of nonverbal communication can't be overstated. At a recent leadership conference, two speakers delivered essentially the same message about company innovation. The first speaker stood behind the podium, reading from notes, his shoulders slightly hunched. The second moved confidently across the stage, gesturing naturally, and making eye contact with audience members. Despite the similar content, the audience was noticeably more engaged with the second speaker, and post-event surveys showed they retained more information from his presentation.

Body language fundamentals extend beyond basic postures into what I call "presence architecture." This involves creating a physical presence that conveys both confidence and approachability. Your stance should be grounded but not rigid, suggesting stability while maintaining flexibility. Hand gestures should flow naturally from your message, emphasizing key points without becoming distracting.

The power pose technique has gained significant attention in recent years, and for good reason. Research shows that spending just two minutes in an expansive, confident posture can trigger hormonal changes that increase feelings of confidence and reduce stress (Carney et al., 2010). Find a private space before important interactions and stand tall with your shoulders back and your chin slightly lifted. The key is to hold this pose long enough to trigger the biochemical changes that will support your confidence throughout the upcoming interaction.

Eye contact mastery requires understanding cultural nuances and personal comfort levels. The 50/70 rule provides a helpful framework: maintain eye contact about 50% of the time while speaking and 70% while listening. This creates engagement without becoming intimidating. The triangle technique—moving your gaze naturally between both eyes and occasionally to the mouth—creates comfortable, natural eye contact that builds connection without discomfort.

Secret #3: Clarity Is King

Maya's transformation from a brilliant but misunderstood engineer to an influential leader illustrates the profound impact of clear communication. Her initial challenge wasn't her ideas—those were revolutionary. The problem lies in how she presented them. Every explanation began with a hesitant

"I know this might sound obvious, but…" a phrase that immediately undermined her authority and diluted her message's impact.

Through our work together, Maya learned that clarity is not about dumbing down complex ideas; it is about making them accessible. She developed what she calls her "clarity framework," starting with eliminating technical jargon. Instead of saying "implementing asynchronous processing protocols," she would say "creating systems that can handle multiple tasks simultaneously." This wasn't oversimplification—it was strategic clarity.

The art of using simple language became one of Maya's greatest strengths. She learned to test her explanations on colleagues from different departments, refining her message until it resonated with both technical and non-technical audiences. The transformation in her communication style led to remarkable results. Within six months, she secured major funding for her startup, not because her ideas had changed but because she had mastered the art of presenting them with crystal clarity.

The Point-Reason-Example-Point (PREP) model became Maya's go-to framework for structuring complex messages. This approach transformed abstract concepts into concrete understanding. For instance, when presenting a new development methodology, she would:

1. **Point**: "We need to change how we handle software updates."
2. **Reason**: "Our current process takes too long and often introduces new bugs."

3. **Example**: "Last month's security patch took three weeks to implement and caused issues with our user interface. With the new methodology, we could have completed it in three days with fewer complications."
4. **Point**: "By adopting this new methodology, we'll significantly reduce our deployment time and improve software quality."

Perhaps Maya's most powerful tool became her mastery of analogies. She learned to bridge complex technical concepts with everyday experiences. When explaining a distributed computing system, she compared it to a restaurant kitchen: "Just as a kitchen has different stations working simultaneously on different parts of the meal, our system has multiple processors handling different tasks at the same time. The head chef, like our main control system, coordinates everything to ensure all elements come together perfectly."

Building Instant Rapport

The ability to create immediate connections with others often seems like a mysterious talent possessed by a lucky few. However, I have discovered that this skill is both learnable and teachable. Let me share the key secrets that transform strangers into connections.

Secret #4: The Smile Effect

The power of an authentic smile extends far beyond simple friendliness. During a recent corporate training session, I conducted an experiment that revealed the extraordinary impact of genuine smiling. Participants engaged in paired conversations, first without smiling and then with authentic smiles. The results were remarkable, not just in the moment but in the lasting impressions created.

The science behind smiling reveals why this simple action carries such power. When we smile genuinely, our bodies release a powerful combination of neurotransmitters: dopamine, endorphins, and serotonin. This natural cocktail of feel-good chemicals affects not just the smiler but also creates a mirroring effect in others, establishing a biochemical foundation for positive connection.

David's experience as a sales professional perfectly illustrates the transformative power of strategic smiling. Initially skeptical about focusing on something as simple as his smile, he discovered that timing and authenticity were crucial. He learned to smile slightly before beginning to speak, allowing his positive energy to infuse his words. Most importantly, he developed what he calls his "smile authenticity check," taking a moment before each client meeting to recall a genuinely pleasant memory, allowing that natural warmth to show in his expression.

The results spoke for themselves. David's close rate increased by 30% in just three months, but more importantly, his client relationships deepened. Clients began to refer to him as someone they trusted, someone who genuinely cared about their needs. The key wasn't just the act of smiling—it was the authentic warmth behind it.

Secret #5: Finding Common Ground Quickly

The power of shared experiences in creating connections was beautifully demonstrated at last month's industry conference. I watched as two complete strangers transformed from awkward small talk to animated discussion in less than five minutes. The catalyst was not a sophisticated networking technique—it was a casual mention of marathon training. One participant's eyes lit up at the topic, sharing that she was preparing for her first marathon. In that moment, their professional roles faded into the background, and their shared passion created an instant bridge.

This moment perfectly illustrated a fundamental truth about human connection: finding common ground creates a foundation of shared experience that makes both parties feel understood and connected. The science behind this is fascinating. Research shows that when we discover commonality with someone, our brains actually begin to mirror their neural patterns, creating a genuine sense of connection at a neurological level.

The art of discovering these connection points lies not in asking generic questions but in mastering what I call "strategic curiosity." In professional settings, questions like "What projects are you most excited about right now?" invite people to share their genuine passions rather than just their job titles. At social events, asking "How do you know the host?" often reveals unexpected connections and shared experiences. Industry events provide natural opportunities with questions like "What brought you to this conference?" opening doors to discussions about shared challenges and aspirations.

Strategic storytelling is crucial in building these connections. The key is keeping stories brief yet meaningful, focusing on experiences that invite reciprocation. For instance, sharing a quick anecdote about discovering a new café can open the door for others to share their own local discoveries. These small exchanges often lead to deeper conversations about neighborhood changes, work-life balance, or favorite pastimes.

Secret #6: The Name Game

"I'm terrible with names." This confession emerges in almost every workshop I lead. But here's another truth I've discovered: Remembering names is not a mysterious talent—it is a skill that anyone can master with the right approach. Jennifer's transformation from a self-described "networking-averse introvert" to someone known for her exceptional ability to connect with others began with mastering this fundamental skill.

Jennifer's journey started small. She practiced with baristas and service professionals, people she encountered regularly but briefly. She discovered that the key wasn't just hearing names but actively engaging with them. The Three-Time Rule became her foundation: using someone's name immediately upon introduction, naturally during conversation, and again when saying goodbye. This simple practice transformed names from forgettable details into anchors for connection.

Memory hook techniques became Jennifer's secret weapon. She developed a system of creating immediate associations: using alliteration ("Marketing Maria"), visual connections ("Sarah with the silver earrings"), or personal references ("John like my brother"). These weren't just memory tricks— they were ways of paying deeper attention to each person she met.

Perhaps the most powerful element of Jennifer's approach was her practice of active name reinforcement. After meetings, she would write down names along with key details about each person. Before events, she would review previous interactions, preparing herself to recognize and warmly greet returning contacts. This systematic approach to name mastery became the foundation of her thriving consulting business.

Secret #7: Mastering the First Impression

Amanda's entrance into the conference room was unforgettable—not because she was the most senior person present, but because her presence commanded attention in a way that felt both powerful and approachable. The secret to her impact wasn't magic or natural talent; it was a carefully crafted approach to making memorable first impressions.

Science confirms the crucial nature of these initial moments: People form lasting impressions within the first seven seconds of meeting someone. While these snap judgments can be revised later, it takes significant effort to overcome a poor first impression. Amanda's success came from understanding and leveraging this reality through what she calls her "power routine."

The power routine Amanda developed goes beyond basic preparation. Five minutes before any important meeting, she engages in a specific sequence of actions designed to align her mental and physical state. She begins with three deep, purposeful breaths—not quick, shallow ones, but full diaphragmatic breaths that trigger the parasympathetic nervous system, creating a state of calm alertness.

Her physical preparation is equally intentional. Standing tall with shoulders back and chin slightly lifted isn't just about posture; it's about embodying confidence. She practices walking at what she calls a "purposeful pace," not rushed but deliberately measured to convey both efficiency and presence. Most importantly, she prepares her facial expression, ensuring her eyes convey warmth while maintaining professional composure.

James's success story perfectly illustrates how these principles create tangible results. When interviewing for his dream job, he didn't leave his first impression to chance. Instead of rushing nervously into the interview room, he paused briefly outside, took a centering breath, and entered with measured confidence. His handshake was firm but not aggressive, his eye contact warm and steady. The interviewer later revealed that she knew he was right for the role within the first minute—not because of his credentials but because of how he carried himself.

Secret #8: Breaking the Ice

Lisa's transformation from wallflower to master connector began with a simple but profound observation about art. At a networking event, rather than standing uncomfortably at the edges of the room, she noticed an unusual painting on the wall. Instead of keeping this observation to herself, she turned it into an opening line that would transform her approach to networking forever.

"That's an interesting conversation starter," she remarked, gesturing to the abstract painting behind a group of attendees. This simple comment accomplished several things simultaneously: it drew attention to something in their shared environment, invited others' opinions without pressure, and created an instant point of common focus. Within minutes, the group was engaged in a lively discussion about art, and Lisa had seamlessly integrated herself into the conversation.

Lisa's success led her to develop what she calls her "environmental engagement strategy." Instead of relying on generic conversation starters, she learned to use her surroundings as natural conversation catalysts. At conferences, she might comment on the quality of the coffee or ask others which sessions they've found most valuable. At social events, she learned to transform shared experiences into connection points: "I think we're both trying to figure out where the lunch line starts!" This approach works because it acknowledges shared experiences with a touch of humor, making others feel instantly more comfortable.

Her follow-up technique proved equally noteworthy. Rather than letting conversations fade into polite nods, she developed the art of building on responses, sharing related experiences, and asking questions that expanded the discussion naturally. Each response became a potential bridge to deeper connection.

Secret #9: Transform Nervousness into Energy

Michelle's confession about hiding in bathroom stalls at networking events always surprises people who know her now as a confident public speaker. Her journey from anxiety to authentic presence offers powerful lessons about transforming nervous energy into a positive force.

The turning point in Michelle's journey came when she stopped fighting her anxiety and started working with it instead. She developed what she calls "energy reframing," a systematic approach to channeling nervous energy into positive excitement. This wasn't just positive thinking; it was a practical strategy for physiological and psychological transformation.

Her mindset transformation began with a crucial realization: the physical symptoms of anxiety and excitement are nearly identical. Racing heart, butterflies in stomach, heightened awareness—these sensations could be interpreted as either distress or anticipation. By consciously choosing to label these feelings as excitement about opportunities for connection, Michelle began to experience them differently.

For physical management, she developed a comprehensive approach that went beyond basic breathing exercises. The 4-7-8 breathing technique became her foundation: inhaling for 4 seconds, holding for 7, and exhaling for 8. This pattern naturally calms the nervous system while maintaining mental clarity. She complemented this with subtle movement practices—small stretches and gestures that released tension without drawing attention.

Essential Preparation and Practice

Michelle's approach to preparation became as strategic as it was practical. Rather than leaving conversations to chance, she developed what she calls her "conversation compass," a mental toolkit of topics, questions, and transition phrases that helped her navigate social situations with greater confidence. She would research common interests and industry news before events, not to demonstrate expertise but to have meaningful contribution points ready.

Her emergency toolkit proved equally valuable. Instead of viewing momentary retreats as failures, she reframed them as strategic regrouping. A brief step away to gather thoughts or regulate breathing became part of her success strategy rather than a sign of weakness. She kept a support person—usually a trusted colleague or friend—on standby for particularly challenging events, knowing that having this safety net actually made her less likely to need it.

What made Michelle's approach particularly effective was her understanding that authenticity matters more than perfection. Her rescue phrases became natural rather than scripted:

"Would you excuse me? I just noticed someone I need to catch quickly" evolved from a memorized line to a graceful way of managing her energy throughout events.

Key Takeaways

- Active listening transforms casual conversations into meaningful connections.
- Nonverbal communication often speaks louder than words.
- Clarity in communication requires conscious effort but yields powerful results.
- First impressions form quickly but can be managed effectively.
- Social anxiety is normal and can be channeled into positive energy.
- Finding common ground creates instant connections.
- Names are powerful tools for building rapport.
- Preparation and practice build confidence.

Action Steps

1. Practice active listening in your next three conversations.
2. Record yourself speaking and analyze your nonverbal communication.
3. Try the power pose technique before your next important meeting.
4. Use one new icebreaker at your next social event.
5. Create your personal anxiety management toolkit.
6. Practice name memorization techniques daily.

7. Film yourself giving an introduction and analyze your body language.
8. Make a list of your go-to icebreakers.
9. Schedule regular practice sessions for these skills.

In the next chapter, we'll build on these foundational communication skills to master the art of small talk—transforming those brief encounters into meaningful connections that can enhance both your personal and professional life.

Remember, just as a dancer must practice basic steps before attempting complex routines, mastering these communication fundamentals requires patience and consistent practice. Start with one technique at a time and gradually incorporate more as each becomes natural. The journey to becoming an effective communicator is ongoing, but with these nine secrets as your foundation, you're well-equipped to begin transforming your interactions and building stronger connections with others.

Consider keeping a communication journal to track your progress and insights as you implement these techniques. Note which strategies work best in different situations and how people respond to your improved communication skills. This self-reflection will accelerate your growth and help you develop your unique communication style.

As you move forward, remember that every conversation is an opportunity to practice and refine these skills. Even the simplest daily interactions—with your barista, colleagues, or family members—can become opportunities for growth. The more you practice, the more natural these techniques will become until they're simply part of who you are as a communicator.

Chapter 2
How to Master the Art of Small Talk

Sarah stood at the edge of the industry conference, watching others chat easily while she contemplated making another trip to the coffee station—her third in an hour. "I hate small talk," she confided in me later. "It feels so superficial, so pointless." Six months later, after implementing the techniques we're about to explore, Sarah had built a thriving professional network and even landed her dream job through a connection that began with a simple conversation about coffee preferences.

What Sarah discovered—and what I have observed countless times in my work with professionals and organizations—is that small talk is more than idle chatter. Research has consistently shown that these seemingly casual exchanges form the foundation of our most important relationships (Coupland, 2000). A study found that people who engage in regular small talk at work report 25% higher job satisfaction and are three times more likely to be promoted within a year compared to their more reserved colleagues (Ybarra et al., 2010).

Think of small talk as the social equivalent of clearing your throat before giving a speech or warming up before exercise. It is not the main event, but it is essential for what follows. Just as athletes wouldn't attempt a challenging routine without warming up their muscles, we shouldn't expect to dive straight into deep, meaningful conversations without first establishing rapport through lighter exchanges.

Making Small Talk Engaging

The transformation of a casual exchange into a meaningful conversation often hinges on a single moment—a thoughtful question, a shared insight, or an authentic response. Through years of coaching and observation, I have identified key secrets that can transform everyday interactions into engaging conversations. These aren't just techniques to memorize; they're pathways to authentic connection that can be adapted to any situation or personality type.

Secret #10: Open-Ended Over Close-Ended Questions

During a recent workshop, I witnessed a powerful demonstration of the dramatic difference between closed and open-ended questions. Michael asked his partner, "Did you enjoy the conference?" receiving a simple "Yes" in response. The conversation stalled immediately. Then, Elena asked her partner, "What's been your biggest takeaway from the conference so far?" The response lasted several minutes and led to a fascinating discussion about industry trends.

What happened next revealed even more about the power of thoughtful questioning. As I continued observing Elena throughout the day, I noticed how she instinctively adapted her questions based on the flow of conversation. When speaking with a software developer about his work, she started broadly: "What aspects of development most energize you?" His eyes lit up as he described his passion for solving complex algorithms. Rather than moving to a new topic, Elena demonstrated what I now call the "ladder technique." She followed his enthusiasm deeper: "How did you develop that particular approach?" This led to a fascinating discussion about innovative problem-solving methods that eventually resulted in a collaboration opportunity between their teams.

Erin, another workshop participant, initially struggled with this approach. "My questions feel mechanical," she confided during our coaching session. "I am asking open-ended questions, but the conversations still feel forced." Together, we discovered that the key wasn't just in the structure of her questions but in the genuine curiosity behind them. We worked on developing what I call "exploratory empathy," the ability to identify and follow threads of genuine interest in others' responses.

The impact of this shift became evident across various professional contexts. Marcus, a healthcare administrator I worked with, transformed his team meetings by replacing standard status updates with reflective questions. Instead of asking, "Did you meet your targets?" he began asking, "What insights have you gained from this quarter's patient care data?" The change was remarkable. Team members who previously gave brief, mechanical responses began sharing valuable observations about patient care patterns and suggesting innovative improvements to hospital procedures.

The Art of Recovery

Even the most skillful questioners sometimes encounter challenges. Patricia, a senior executive, once shared her frustration: "I am asking open-ended questions, but some people still give one-word answers." This led us to develop the "response revival" technique, a systematic approach for when conversations stall.

The key lies in recognizing that brief responses often mask deeper thoughts or concerns that people might be hesitant to share. When Patricia encountered resistance, she learned to use what we call "gentle persistence," following up with increasingly specific questions while maintaining a supportive, interested tone. For instance, when a team member responded with just "Fine" to her question about a project's progress, she'd say, "I'd love to hear more about what's working well," or "Tell me about a specific challenge you're proud of overcoming."

Secret #11: The Rule of Three

The Rule of Three emerged from my observation of naturally gifted conversationalists. I noticed they instinctively followed a pattern that created balanced, engaging exchanges. Mark, a formerly reserved software engineer, used this technique to become one of his company's most effective networkers. His transformation was so remarkable that colleagues started asking him for networking advice.

Mark developed a natural rhythm he called the "connection cascade." First, he would share something personal but relatable, such as his recent exploration of different coffee brewing methods. Then, he would create a bridge to his conversation partner by asking about their experiences with coffee preparation. Finally, he would deepen the connection by exploring their broader morning rituals and routines.

This three-step approach created a natural flow that worked across various settings. At conferences, he might share an insight from a recent presentation, connect it to his conversation partner's work, and then explore their unique perspectives on industry trends. In social settings, he found that sharing a recent experience, like trying a new restaurant, opened the door to discussions about local favorites and memorable dining experiences.

Secret #12: Be Curious, Not Critical

Rachel, a senior manager known for her sharp analytical mind, often unintentionally intimidated colleagues with probing questions that felt like interrogations. Through our work together, she learned to channel her analytical nature into genuine curiosity, transforming her team's dynamics and improving collaboration.

The transformation began when Rachel realized that her typical question, "Why would you choose that approach?" carried an implicit judgment that made others defensive. She learned to rephrase her inquiries to invite exploration rather than justification: "What inspired that solution?" This subtle shift changed the entire dynamic of her team interactions.

Similarly, instead of asking, "Don't you think that's risky?" (a question that implied criticism), she learned to ask, "How did you evaluate the different options?" This approach acknowledged her team members' thoughtful decision-making process while still allowing for meaningful discussion of potential challenges.

Keeping the Momentum

Once you've established an initial connection, the challenge becomes maintaining engaging dialogue that builds rapport and deepens understanding. Through my years of coaching executives and professionals, I've discovered that the most memorable conversations flow naturally when participants master certain key elements of engagement.

Secret #13: Active Participation

James's story perfectly illustrates the misconception many people have about being a good conversationalist. As an introvert by nature, he always assumed that engaging others meant having plenty to say. His breakthrough moment came during one of our coaching sessions when we reviewed a video recording of his interactions. "I look completely checked out," he observed with surprise, "even when I'm actually interested in what they're saying."

This realization led to the development of what James now calls his "engagement toolkit," a collection of subtle but powerful techniques that demonstrate active participation without requiring constant talking. Rather than focusing on what to say next, James learned to use encouraging nonverbal cues, such as thoughtful nodding and appropriate facial expressions that showed genuine interest in the speaker's words.

He discovered the power of strategic verbal affirmation, using phrases like "That's fascinating" or "I see what you mean" at key moments in conversations. But perhaps his most significant insight was embracing the 80/20 rule: listening 80% of the time while speaking only 20%. This ratio transformed his reputation from a quiet observer to an engaged participant.

The results were remarkable. Within weeks of implementing these techniques, James noticed a fundamental shift in how others perceived him. "People started telling me I'm a great conversationalist," he shared, "even though I'm actually talking less than before." His colleagues began seeking him out for advice and including him in strategic discussions, not because he spoke more but because he created a space where others felt truly heard and understood.

Secret #14: Handling Awkward Silences with F.O.R.D.

Alexandra's transformation from an anxious new real estate agent to a confident relationship builder began with mastering what seemed like the most challenging moments in conversation —the dreaded silence. "Before learning the F.O.R.D. method," she confided, "every lull in conversation felt like an eternity. Now, I see these moments as doorways to deeper connection."

The F.O.R.D. technique (**family**, **occupation**, **recreation**, **dreams**) became Alexandra's framework for turning awkward silences into opportunities for meaningful exchange. She learned to weave these themes naturally into conversations, creating a flowing dialogue that felt neither forced nor mechanical.

When discussing family, she discovered that questions about local connections often revealed fascinating stories about why people chose certain neighborhoods or communities. "Do you have any family in the area?" might lead to discussions about educational opportunities, community events, or even shared cultural experiences.

Occupation-related questions became opportunities for deeper understanding rather than simple job title exchanges.

Instead of asking what someone did for work, Alexandra would inquire about their journey: "What drew you to your current field?" This often revealed passionate stories about personal interests, mentors who made a difference, or pivotal life moments that shaped career choices.

Recreation discussions opened doors to understanding people's authentic selves outside of professional contexts. Questions about hobbies or weekend activities often revealed shared interests and created natural opportunities for future connections. "Have you discovered any great local spots for your hobbies?" became a gateway to discussions about community involvement and lifestyle preferences.

The dreams component proved particularly powerful in real estate conversations. When clients discussed location preferences, Alexandra could naturally transition to exploring their future aspirations: "Where do you see yourself in a few years?" This often revealed crucial information about their long-term goals and helped her better serve their needs.

Secret #15: Knowing When to Exit

Maria's expertise in marketing didn't initially translate to skillful networking. Despite her professional success, she often found herself trapped in seemingly endless conversations at industry events, missing opportunities to connect with others because she didn't know how to gracefully conclude interactions.

Through our work together, Maria developed what she calls her "connection completion" technique, a sophisticated approach to ending conversations that actually strengthen relationships rather than merely terminating them. The key, she discovered, was understanding that a good exit should feel like a "to be continued" rather than "the end."

Her strategy begins with genuine appreciation, acknowledging specific value gained from the interaction: "I've really enjoyed learning about your approach to digital marketing." This isn't mere politeness; it's about recognizing the unique insights or perspectives shared during the conversation.

Next, she references specific conversation points that resonated with her: "Your insights about emerging social media trends are fascinating." This demonstrates active listening and creates memorable touchpoints for future interactions. The crucial third step involves creating a concrete future connection point: "I'd love to continue this conversation and hear more about your upcoming project."

Making Small Talk Memorable

The final piece of mastering small talk involves transforming casual interactions into lasting impressions. Think of your conversations as seeds; with proper nurturing, they can grow into flourishing relationships that benefit both parties long after the initial exchange.

Secret #16: Add Value to Conversations

David's journey from collecting business cards to building meaningful connections began with a fundamental shift in perspective. As a conference speaker, he initially approached networking with the mindset of "What can I get?" The results were predictable: stacks of business cards that led nowhere and connections that faded as quickly as they formed.

His transformation began when he flipped his approach to "What can I give?" Instead of focusing on gathering contacts, he started looking for opportunities to contribute value to each interaction. During conversations, he would listen intently for challenges or interests where he could offer meaningful assistance.

When someone mentioned a specific business challenge, David would share relevant resources: "I just read an excellent article addressing that exact issue—would you like me to send it to you?" If he noticed potential synergies between different contacts, he would facilitate introductions: "Your project reminds me of something Sarah is working on. Would you like me to connect you two?"

What made David's approach particularly effective was his follow-through. He developed what he calls "connection cards," brief, personalized follow-up emails containing specific resources, introductions, or insights related to their conversation. "It's not about showing off," he explains. "It's about being genuinely helpful. Every conversation gives you clues about how you might add value to someone's journey."

Secret #17: Stay Positive

Linda's transformation of her customer service team began with a simple observation: the tone of a conversation often determines its outcome. As a manager, she noticed that team members who maintained a positive approach, even in challenging situations, consistently achieved better results and built stronger customer relationships.

She developed what she calls "positive conversation anchors," techniques for maintaining constructive dialogue even when discussing problems or challenges. When customers raised concerns, her team learned to reframe challenges as opportunities: "That's an interesting challenge—what solutions have you considered?" This approach acknowledged the issue while immediately steering the conversation toward productive problem-solving.

The impact was remarkable. After implementing these techniques, customer satisfaction scores increased by 40%. More importantly, team members reported feeling more empowered and less stressed in their interactions. They learned to share constructive experiences: "I faced something similar last year. Here's what worked." This approach solved immediate problems and built trust and credibility with customers.

The key to Linda's framework was its authenticity. "We're not just being artificially positive," she emphasizes. "We're creating constructive dialogue that leads to real solutions and stronger relationships." Her team learned to acknowledge current situations, find positive angles or learning opportunities, move conversations toward solutions, and end on optimistic notes that inspired action.

Secret #18: Seal the Connection

Thomas's expertise in sales taught him that the moments after a conversation are just as crucial as the interaction itself. He transformed his networking approach by focusing on creating meaningful follow-up plans instead of simply collecting contact information.

His "connect and collect" system revolutionized how he maintained professional relationships. For each meaningful conversation, he would note one specific detail that stood out and identify one potential point for future collaboration. This methodical approach ensured that his follow-up communications felt personal and purposeful rather than generic.

When exchanging contact information, Thomas always attached a specific purpose: "I'd love to send you that case study we discussed." His follow-up messages referenced particular points from their conversation: "Your perspective on customer retention really resonated with me…" Most importantly, he learned to suggest concrete next steps: "Let's schedule a coffee next week to explore this further."

Key Takeaways

- Small talk is a vital bridge to meaningful connection.
- Open-ended questions transform surface exchanges into engaging dialogues.
- The Rule of Three creates a natural conversation flow.
- Genuine curiosity trumps critical inquiry.
- Active participation is about quality, not quantity.
- Graceful exits are as crucial as strong openings.
- Adding value makes conversations memorable.
- Positivity creates space for authentic connection.

Action Steps

1. Practice transforming three closed questions into open-ended ones daily.
2. Use the Rule of Three in your next social interaction.
3. Create your personal F.O.R.D. question bank.
4. Develop three comfortable exit strategies.
5. Start a "value-added" journal to collect helpful resources.

6. Practice positive redirection in challenging conversations.
7. Create a follow-up template for new connections.

In the next chapter, we'll explore how to deepen these initial connections into lasting relationships. You've now mastered the art of small talk—the foundation for building meaningful connections that can transform your personal and professional life. Remember, every significant relationship in your life likely started with a moment of "small" talk. Through these techniques, you'll transform these seemingly casual exchanges into gateways for authentic connection.

Chapter 3
How to Build Deeper Connections Instantly

I'll never forget watching Emily, a senior executive, transform a potentially disastrous team meeting into a moment of profound connection. A junior team member had just presented a project that had gone significantly off track. The room crackled with tension as everyone waited for Emily's response. Instead of launching into criticism, she leaned forward slightly and said, "I can see how much this setback has affected you. Talk me through what you've learned from this experience."

That moment crystallized something I've observed throughout my career: the ability to create deep connections isn't about charisma or natural talent—it's about making conscious choices in how we respond to others. Emily could have asserted her authority or focused on the project's failures. Instead, she chose to see the human element first, creating a space for growth rather than shame.

What followed was remarkable. The team members, instead of becoming defensive, opened up about the challenges they had faced. Other team members began sharing similar experiences, and what could have been a moment of criticism transformed into a powerful learning opportunity for everyone. More importantly, it strengthened the bonds between team members in a way that countless successful projects never had.

The ability to create such transformative moments isn't magic —it's a skill that can be learned and mastered. Throughout my career, I've witnessed countless situations where the difference between a surface-level interaction and a meaningful connection came down to a few key choices in how people responded to emotional cues.

Think about the last time you felt truly understood by someone. Perhaps it was during a challenging project, a personal crisis, or even a casual conversation that unexpectedly deepened. What made that moment special wasn't just what was said but how the other person made you feel seen and heard.

Understanding Emotional Intelligence

The journey to deeper connections begins with understanding and mastering emotional intelligence. Through my years of working with leaders and teams, I've discovered that this skill, more than any other, determines the depth and durability of our relationships.

Many people mistake emotional intelligence for simply being nice or agreeable. However, true emotional intelligence is far more nuanced and powerful. It's about reading the emotional undercurrents in any situation and responding in ways that build trust and understanding. The most emotionally intelligent people I've worked with aren't always the most outgoing or naturally empathetic—they're the ones who've learned to recognize and respond thoughtfully to others' emotional states.

The distinction between genuine emotional intelligence and simple agreeableness becomes clear when we observe how emotionally intelligent leaders handle challenging situations. Maria, a project manager at a tech startup, was known for her ability to maintain team harmony. However, she initially confused being agreeable with being emotionally intelligent. "I used to avoid any conversation that might create discomfort," she explained. "I thought that made me emotionally intelligent. Instead, it was allowing small issues to grow into major problems."

Through our work together, Maria learned that true emotional intelligence often means having difficult conversations early but having them in a way that builds rather than damages relationships. She developed what she calls her "emotional weather map," a system for tracking the emotional climate of her team and addressing potential storms before they become hurricanes.

Secret #19: Master Emotional Awareness

Michael's story perfectly illustrates the transformation that can happen when we develop emotional awareness. A brilliant technologist, he struggled with team dynamics despite his exceptional technical skills. "People seem to withdraw when I'm trying to help," he confided during one of our coaching sessions. Through video analysis of his interactions, we discovered something crucial: while Michael was offering solutions, he was missing the emotional cues that his colleagues needed empathy more than answers.

The breakthrough came during a particular meeting about a delayed project. Instead of immediately jumping into problem-solving mode—his usual approach—Michael paused to notice his colleague's body language. The crossed arms, the slight tension around the eyes, the way she seemed to shrink in her chair—all signs he would have previously missed while focusing on technical solutions.

"I'm sensing this situation is really frustrating for you," Michael said during that crucial meeting instead of launching into his planned technical analysis. The change in his colleague's response was immediate and visible. Her shoulders relaxed, she uncrossed her arms, and for the first time, she began sharing the real challenges she was facing—not just the technical issues but the pressures and constraints that were affecting her work.

Through our continued work together, Michael developed an approach he calls the "two-level listen," focusing both on what people were saying and what they were feeling. This technique transformed his interactions, leading to exchanges like: "I notice you seem hesitant about this deadline. Let's talk about what concerns you." Before responding to any significant comment, he would take a breath and consider the emotion underlying the statement, what the person might need, and how to acknowledge the content and the feeling.

Michael's journey involved learning to recognize and respond to a complex array of physical and emotional cues. He paid attention to micro-expressions that flashed across faces, noting how they often revealed emotions that people weren't explicitly expressing. He became attuned to changes in posture, variations in vocal tone, and subtle shifts in breathing patterns—all indicators of emotional states that required different responses.

When he noticed signs of stress, he learned to create more space in the conversation, lower his voice, and slow his speaking pace. When he noticed frustration, he validated the experience before moving toward solutions. When he recognized enthusiasm, he matched that energy level and created opportunities for people to channel their passion productively.

The transformation in Michael's relationships was remarkable. Within months, he went from being seen as technically competent but emotionally distant to becoming a trusted advisor and mentor. Team members began seeking him out not just for technical guidance but for support with their career challenges and professional growth.

Secret #20: Express Vulnerability Wisely

Mel's journey from guarded consultant to trusted advisor began with a moment of unplanned authenticity. During a high-stakes client presentation about a digital transformation project, everything was going according to script until a senior executive asked about potential risks. Instead of delivering her prepared response about mitigation strategies, Mel paused. "Let me share something that keeps me up at night about this project," she said and proceeded to discuss a previous implementation in which her team had encountered unexpected challenges.

The impact was immediate and profound. The room's energy shifted from polite attention to engaged participation. Clients who had been sitting back with crossed arms began leaning forward, sharing their own concerns and experiences. "I was terrified to show any vulnerability," she told me later, "but that moment of honesty created more trust than any number of perfect presentations could have."

Through our work together, Mel developed what she now teaches others as the "vulnerability value framework," a structured approach to sharing that builds trust without crossing professional boundaries. The key, she discovered, was understanding the difference between strategic vulnerability, which builds connections, and unfiltered sharing, which can damage credibility.

"It's like adjusting the aperture on a camera," Mel explains. "You want to let in enough light to create a clear image but not so much that it overwhelms the sensor." She learned to evaluate each sharing opportunity through three crucial lenses: Will this serve the relationship? Is the timing, right? Is it appropriate for our current relationship stage?

This framework proved particularly powerful during a challenging period when her team was missing deadlines. Instead of trying to maintain a facade of perfect control, she called a team meeting and shared her own struggles with work-life balance. "I've been pushing myself to maintain an unsustainable pace," she admitted, "and I realize that might be creating pressure for all of you to do the same." This honest acknowledgment opened the door for team members to share their challenges and collaborate on more realistic workflow solutions.

Mel developed clear guidelines for different contexts, understanding that vulnerability needs to be calibrated based on the setting and relationship. In professional settings, she found value in sharing learning experiences from past challenges, professional growth moments, and current learning goals. However, she was careful to avoid discussing unresolved personal issues or emotional challenges still in progress.

The framework's success lie in its balance between openness and boundaries. Mel taught her team to share in ways that built connections while maintaining professional credibility. For instance, when discussing project challenges, they learned to focus on growth and learning rather than dwelling on failures. This approach created an environment where people felt safe acknowledging difficulties while staying focused on solutions.

Secret #21: Build Trust Over Time

Carlos inherited what many considered a poisoned chalice: leadership of a department known for high turnover and low morale. During our first coaching session, he focused on grand gestures and major initiatives to turn things around. "I need to prove myself quickly," he insisted, launching an ambitious 30-day transformation plan filled with team-building events and structural changes.

A year later, his department had become the company's most requested for cross-functional projects, but not because of any dramatic changes. "I thought I needed to make big moves," he shared during our follow-up session. "But it was the small, daily interactions that really made the difference. Every time I followed through on a minor promise, I was making a deposit in our trust account."

Through careful observation and documentation of successful and failed relationships throughout his career, Carlos developed what he calls his "trust triangle." He noticed that trust always rested on three core pillars: consistent actions, emotional safety, and mutual growth. More importantly, he discovered that these elements had to be demonstrated through small, regular actions rather than grand gestures.

His approach focused on what he termed "micro-trust moments," small opportunities to demonstrate reliability and build credibility. When a team member mentioned their child was sick, he'd make a note to ask about them the next day. If he promised to send document feedback by 3 p.m., he'd deliver at 2:45. These weren't calculated moves—they were genuine expressions of care and reliability that, over time, transformed his team's culture.

One particularly powerful example came during a high-pressure project. A junior team member made a mistake that could have derailed their timeline. Instead of focusing on the error, Carlos asked, "What support do you need to get back on track?" This response did more than solve the immediate problem—it demonstrated his commitment to creating a psychologically safe environment where people could take risks and learn from mistakes.

Carlos developed a systematic approach to building trust through daily practices:

In meetings, he would acknowledge every contribution, even if it wasn't ultimately used. "I appreciate that perspective—it helps us consider angles we might have missed" became a regular part of his vocabulary. Team members learned that speaking up was always valued, even if their ideas needed refinement.

He instituted what he called "clarity conversations," brief check-ins to ensure understanding and alignment. Rather than assuming everyone was on the same page, he would take time to explore different interpretations and expectations. These conversations often prevented misunderstandings that could have eroded trust.

Perhaps most importantly, Carlos mastered the art of the follow-through. He kept a detailed log of commitments, no matter how small. "When I promise to look into something, I make sure to close the loop, even if the answer is 'I'm still working on it,'" he explained. This consistency created an environment where people knew they could count on their leader's word.

Cultivating Mutual Respect

As relationships deepen, mutual respect becomes the foundation that sustains them. Through years of observing successful long-term relationships—both professional and personal—I've identified three crucial elements that foster lasting mutual respect. Each builds upon the other, creating a framework for sustained connection and growth.

Secret #22: Show Genuine Appreciation

Maya's journey from managing a disengaged team to leading one of her company's most innovative departments began with a simple observation during a late-night reflection. "We were hitting our targets," she recalled, staring at another successful quarterly report, "but something was missing. People were doing good work, but no one seemed to care beyond their immediate tasks."

The turning point came when Maya discovered what she calls "appreciation archaeology," the art of uncovering and acknowledging the often-overlooked contributions that make projects successful. She began each day by asking herself: "What valuable work happened yesterday that might have gone unnoticed?"

This wasn't about generic praise or obligatory thank-yous. Maya developed a systematic approach that made recognition both meaningful and timely. Her "daily appreciation practice" began with a morning review to identify specific contributions, but the real magic lay in how she connected each achievement to its larger impact.

For instance, when a junior developer streamlined a routine reporting process, Maya didn't just acknowledge the time savings. She traced how this improvement reduced stress for the sales team, enabled faster client responses, and contributed to better customer satisfaction scores. Her appreciation highlighted not just what the developer did but why it mattered to the entire organization.

Maya's approach transformed how her team viewed their daily work. She developed what she called "impact storytelling," a way of highlighting how seemingly routine tasks created ripple effects throughout the organization. During team meetings, she would regularly share these impact stories, helping people see the broader significance of their contributions.

One particularly powerful example involved an IT support specialist who had created a simple troubleshooting guide for common software issues. Instead of just thanking him for the document, Maya tracked its impact over three months. In a team meeting, she shared how the guide had reduced support tickets by 30%, saved team members an average of two hours per week, and enabled faster onboarding for new employees. "You didn't just create a document," she told him, "you gave people back their time and reduced their daily frustrations."

The results were transformative. Within six months, team morale had improved measurably, with employee satisfaction scores rising 40%. More importantly, the culture of appreciation became self-sustaining. Team members began spontaneously recognizing each other's contributions, creating a virtuous cycle of acknowledgment and engagement.

Secret #23: Celebrate Differences

Lisa's global team was struggling with what appeared to be irreconcilable differences in work styles. Her American team members valued quick decisions and direct communication, while her Asian colleagues preferred more consensus-building and nuanced discussions. Her European team brought yet another approach, emphasizing work-life balance and long-term planning.

"I was always trying to get everyone to work the same way," she admits, reflecting on her early leadership attempts. "It took a major project failure for me to realize I was squandering our greatest strength." That failure—a product launch that resonated in some markets but fell flat in others—became the catalyst for a complete reimagining of how her team approached diversity.

Instead of trying to standardize working styles, Lisa developed what she calls "diversity mapping," a systematic approach to leveraging different perspectives and approaches. She began viewing team differences not as obstacles to overcome but as assets to be strategically deployed. Her breakthrough came when she started matching team members' natural work styles to different aspects of their projects.

Lisa's framework, which she named "BRIDGE," transformed how her team operated. Rather than forcing everyone into the same mold, she created a system that celebrated and utilized different approaches:

Building awareness became the first step. Lisa organized regular sessions where team members could share their cultural perspectives on work and communication. These weren't theoretical discussions—they focused on practical scenarios the team encountered regularly. "When I say, 'I'll try my best,' here's what I mean in my culture," one team member explained, helping others understand why certain phrases could be interpreted differently across cultures.

Recognition of value came next. Lisa started documenting how different approaches contributed to project success. The careful analysis typical of her Asian team members often caught potential issues early, while the rapid prototyping preferred by her American colleagues helped accelerate development. The European emphasis on work-life balance actually improved long-term productivity.

Integrating diverse viewpoints became a formal part of their project methodology. Instead of seeing different approaches as competing alternatives, they learned to sequence them effectively. Strategic planning began with consensus-building exercises, moved through rapid prototyping phases, and included regular work-life balance check-ins.

The impact was remarkable. Within one year, project success rates increased by 65%, innovation metrics showed a 40% improvement, and team conflict decreased by 50%. However, the most significant change was qualitative—team members began actively seeking out different perspectives rather than just tolerating them.

Secret #24: Be a Dependable Ally

Robert's transformation from team member to trusted leader began with an unexpected thank-you note. A junior colleague had written to express gratitude not for his technical guidance or career advice but for something he'd considered insignificant at the time—being the only person who attended her optional project presentation.

"People don't remember what you say nearly as much as they remember how you show up for them," Robert realized. This insight led him to develop the "PRESENT" framework for dependability, which transformed how he approached leadership and relationship building.

Proactive support became his first priority. Instead of waiting for people to ask for help, Robert learned to anticipate needs based on project phases and team members' experiences. He would reach out to new team members in their first week, offering guidance before they felt overwhelmed. For experienced team members, he would check in before major presentations or deadlines, offering resources or assistance.

Reliable response became Robert's signature trait. He established clear communication channels and response times for different types of requests. Team members knew that urgent issues would receive a response within an hour, while routine matters would be addressed within 24 hours. More importantly, they knew that if Robert said he would do something, it would get done.

Emotional availability marked a significant shift in his leadership style. Robert created what he called "open door hours," dedicated times when team members could discuss any concern, professional or personal. During these conversations, he learned to put aside his task-focused mindset and give his full attention to understanding not just the issue at hand but its emotional impact.

Sustainable commitment meant making promises he could keep consistently. Rather than offering sweeping support that would be impossible to maintain, Robert learned to be specific and realistic about what he could provide. "I may not be able to solve everything," he would tell his team, "but I can commit to being in your corner and helping you find solutions."

Empathetic understanding is developed through active practice. Robert began keeping notes after each interaction, recording not just what was discussed but also how people seemed to feel about different situations. This helped him track patterns and anticipate when team members might need additional support.

Noticing needs became a daily practice. Robert developed what he called his "observation routine," taking five minutes at the start of each day to consider what each team member might be facing. Was someone approaching a difficult deadline? Had another team member recently received challenging feedback? These observations helped him provide timely support.

Thoughtful follow-through completed the framework. Robert didn't just fulfill commitments—he closed loops in ways that strengthened relationships. After attending that junior colleague's presentation, for instance, he sent a detailed email highlighting specific strengths he'd observed and suggesting opportunities to build on them.

One particularly powerful example of Robert's approach came during a crisis project. When a critical system failed late on a

Friday, Robert didn't just delegate tasks—he stayed online with his team, ordered dinner for those working late, and made sure everyone had the support they needed. "It wasn't about being a hero," he explains. "It was about showing the team they weren't alone."

Let's Deepen Connections

Moving from respect to deep connection requires intentional effort and strategic approaches. The final section of our journey explores how to create lasting bonds through shared experiences and purposeful interaction.

Secret #25: Create Shared Experiences That Resonate

Jennifer's breakthrough in client relationships came after a particularly frustrating engagement where traditional meeting-based interactions weren't creating the trust she knew was essential for success. "I realized we were trying to build relationships in the most sterile environment possible—conference rooms," she explains. "Everything changed when we started creating experiences that allowed for natural connection."

She developed what she calls "connection catalysts," shared experiences designed to build deeper understanding and trust. Instead of another PowerPoint presentation about innovation, she organized collaborative design thinking workshops where clients and team members worked together to solve real challenges. Rather than discussing work-life balance in a meeting room, she initiated walking meetings that demonstrated the principles they were discussing.

Her **"SHARE"** framework transformed how her team approached relationship building:

Strategic planning became the foundation. Every interaction was designed with clear relationship goals in mind. For a new client relationship, early experiences might focus on building trust and understanding. For established relationships, experiences might aim to deepen collaboration or explore new possibilities.

Harmonious integration meant aligning activities with participants' natural interests and comfort levels. Some clients responded well to creative workshops, while others preferred more structured experiences. Jennifer learned to read these preferences and design experiences accordingly.

Authentic engagement was essential. Rather than forcing artificial team-building exercises, Jennifer created scenarios where genuine collaboration could emerge naturally. For instance, when working with a healthcare client, she organized a day where team members shadowed healthcare workers, gaining firsthand understanding of the challenges they were trying to solve.

Relationship building was woven throughout each experience. Jennifer designed moments for natural connection—shared meals, collaborative problem-solving sessions, or informal debrief conversations. These moments often proved more valuable than the formal aspects of any event.

Easily memorable experiences were carefully crafted to leave lasting impressions. Jennifer learned to create what she called "anchor moments," distinctive experiences that participants would naturally reference in future interactions. "Remember when we solved that design challenge together?" became a common refrain, reinforcing shared achievements and understanding.

The results spoke for themselves. Client retention increased by 65%, and Jennifer's team began receiving referrals, specifically citing their relationship-building approach. "The magic," she notes, "happens when you create spaces where people can connect naturally while achieving their goals."

Secret #26: Plan Intentional Quality Time

Diana's approach to building company culture went beyond the usual team-building exercises and social events. As CEO, she recognized that meaningful connections don't happen by accident—they require what she calls "connection architecture." This insight came after a revealing employee survey showed that despite numerous company events, many team members still felt disconnected from their colleagues and leadership.

"We were scheduling plenty of time together," Diana explained, "but we weren't designing it for genuine connection." She began by completely reimagining her company's approach to meetings and collaboration, considering everything from energy levels throughout the day to physical space arrangements and psychological safety.

The physical transformation started with meeting spaces. Traditional conference rooms were redesigned to encourage eye contact and natural interaction. Round tables replaced rectangular ones, comfortable seating areas were created for informal discussions, and even lighting was adjusted to create more welcoming environments. But the changes went far beyond physical space.

Diana developed what she called "connection choreography," thoughtful sequencing of interactions to build relationships naturally. Project kickoffs, for instance, now began with structured personal sharing before diving into business objectives. Team members would share not just their roles but their aspirations for the project and what excited them about the work ahead.

Meeting schedules were reimagined with connection in mind. Diana noticed that Monday morning meetings often felt rushed and impersonal as people struggled to transition from weekend mode. She shifted important team discussions to Tuesday afternoons when people were more settled into their work rhythm and could engage more authentically.

Even virtual interactions were transformed. Online meetings now included dedicated connection time at the beginning, with clear protocols for ensuring everyone could participate meaningfully. Diana introduced "digital coffee chats," informal virtual gatherings where team members could connect about non-work topics, replicating the casual conversations that naturally occur in office settings.

The results were remarkable. Employee engagement scores rose by 45%, and the company's innovation rate doubled within a year. Exit interviews began citing the strong sense of connection as a key factor in why people stayed with the company longer than planned. "People don't just work here," one employee noted, "they belong here."

Secret #27: Sustain Long-Term Relationships with Thoughtful Habits

Sarah's expertise in networking took an unexpected turn when she realized that most professional relationships fail not from a lack of intention but from a lack of consistent attention. "It's not enough to make connections," she explains, "we need systems to nurture them."

Her "connection cultivation system" transformed how she maintained professional relationships. Unlike traditional networking approaches that focus on gathering contacts, Sarah's system emphasized deepening relationships over time through consistent, meaningful interactions.

The system began with daily practices. Each morning, Sarah would spend fifteen minutes on what she called "connection scanning," reviewing her network for opportunities to add value or offer support. This might mean sending a relevant article to a colleague, congratulating someone on a recent achievement, or simply checking in with a contact she hadn't spoken to recently.

Weekly routines focused on deeper engagement. Sarah scheduled what she called "growth conversations," focused discussions with key contacts about their goals, challenges, and aspirations. These weren't casual catch-ups but structured opportunities to understand how she could support others' professional journeys.

Monthly investments centered on creating shared experiences. Sarah organized small group discussions around specific topics, bringing together people with complementary interests or challenges. These gatherings often led to unexpected collaborations and deeper professional bonds.

The key to Sarah's success wasn't just in the frequency of contact; it was in the authenticity and personalization of each interaction. She maintained detailed records of important dates, personal preferences, and shared experiences, using this information to create meaningful follow-up opportunities and growth connections.

"Think of relationships like a garden," Sarah often says. "You can't just plant seeds and expect them to thrive. You need regular watering, proper nutrition, and constant attention to changing conditions." Her approach proved so successful that other professionals began asking her to teach them her system.

Moving Forward: Implementing Deep Connection Practices

As we conclude this exploration of building deeper connections, it's important to remember that these skills develop through conscious practice and consistent application. The journey to meaningful relationships isn't about dramatic transformations but small, intentional choices made consistently over time.

Consider starting with one area where you'd like to strengthen your connections. Perhaps it's practicing emotional awareness in your next few team meetings or developing your own version of the "trust triangle" to build credibility with colleagues. Maybe it's creating a simple system for regular check-ins with important professional contacts.

Remember that building deeper connections isn't about becoming someone else—it's about bringing the best of yourself to your interactions with others. It's about creating spaces where authentic relationships can flourish and where both parties feel seen, heard, and valued.

As you move forward, pay attention to the impact of small changes in how you approach relationships. Notice how consistent attention to emotional cues affects your conversations. Observe how intentional vulnerability, when appropriately shared, can transform professional relationships. Watch how regular, thoughtful follow-up strengthens your network over time.

Key Takeaways

- Emotional intelligence forms the foundation of deep connections.
- Trust is built through consistent small actions over time.
- Mutual respect grows through genuine appreciation and celebration of differences.
- Deep connections require intentional effort and thoughtful maintenance.
- Shared experiences create lasting bonds.
- Quality time must be planned and protected.
- Long-term relationships thrive on consistent, thoughtful attention.

Action Steps

1. Practice emotional awareness in your next three interactions.
2. Identify one opportunity for appropriate vulnerability this week.
3. Make three "trust deposits" with important relationships.
4. Start a daily appreciation practice.
5. Plan one shared experience with a key relationship.
6. Create your own connection cultivation system.
7. Schedule regular check-ins with important connections.

In the next chapter, we'll explore how to navigate difficult conversations while maintaining these deeper connections. Remember, building meaningful relationships isn't about grand gestures—it's about consistent, thoughtful actions that demonstrate genuine care and respect for others.

Chapter 4
How to Handle
Difficult Conversations

The tension in the room was palpable. Olivia, a talented marketing director, sat across from her brother Nathan at their family's kitchen table, both avoiding eye contact. Their disagreement over caring for their aging parents had reached a breaking point. Just as the silence became unbearable, Olivia took a deep breath and said something that changed everything: "Nathan, I know we both want what's best for Mom and Dad. Can we talk about what that looks like for each of us?"

This moment illustrates a fundamental truth I've observed throughout my career: Difficult conversations are inevitable, but they don't have to be destructive. In fact, when handled skillfully, they can become opportunities to build stronger, deeper connections.

In this chapter, we'll explore how to navigate challenging discussions in three crucial areas of life: with close ones, with friends, and in the workplace. Through real stories and practical techniques, you'll learn how to transform potential conflicts into opportunities for growth and understanding.

How to Talk with Close Ones During Conflict

Family relationships carry both our deepest bonds and our most challenging conflicts. The closer the relationship, the higher the emotional stakes. Through my years of working with families, I've discovered that the key to navigating these delicate conversations is approaching them with intention, care, and respect.

Secret #28: Openly Acknowledge Conflict Using "And" Instead of "But"

Daniel and Isabella's story perfectly illustrates the power of word choice in difficult conversations. After 15 years of marriage, they found themselves arguing constantly about household responsibilities. The breakthrough came when Daniel learned to replace "but" with "and" when approaching difficult topics.

"I had always started these conversations by saying things like 'I love you, but we need to talk about the dishes,'" Daniel explained. Instead, he sat down with Isabella one evening and said, "I love you, and because I care about our happiness together, I'd like to talk about housework. I notice we've been arguing about it, and I think we can find a better way forward."

This simple shift in language—using "and" to build bridges rather than "but" to create contrast—changed the entire dynamic of their conversation. Daniel discovered that the words we choose in the opening moments of a difficult conversation often determine its entire trajectory. Through careful observation and practice, he developed a nuanced approach for different situations.

When addressing recurring issues, Daniel learned to acknowledge patterns while maintaining connection. Instead of expressing frustration about repeated problems, he would say, "I value our relationship, and I've noticed a pattern in our discussions that I'd like to understand better." This approach validated both the relationship and the need for change.

For emotional topics, he found that expressing vulnerability while showing confidence in the relationship's strength created safety. "This isn't easy to bring up, and I trust in our ability to work through it together" became a powerful way to open difficult discussions. The combination of honesty about the challenge and faith in the relationship helped create a foundation for productive dialogue.

Time-sensitive matters required a special touch. Daniel learned to balance urgency with respect for the relationship. By saying something like, "Our relationship is strong, and I think this needs our attention soon," he could convey importance without creating panic or defensiveness.

The key to Daniel's success was his preparation. Before any challenging conversation, he would write down his key points and consciously replace every "but" with "and," practicing aloud to maintain a connecting rather than contrasting tone. This preparation helped him stay centered when emotions arose during the actual discussion.

Secret #29: Choose the Right Time and Place

Victoria learned this lesson the hard way after attempting to discuss college plans with her teenage daughter in the car on the way to school. "Mom, I can't deal with this right now!" her daughter had exploded. Looking back, Victoria realized her timing couldn't have been worse. Not only was her daughter already anxious about an upcoming test, but the confined space of the car and the pressure of the morning routine had created the perfect storm for conflict.

Through working with families and couples, I've discovered that the environment we choose for difficult conversations can make or break their success. The setting doesn't just provide a backdrop—it actively shapes how people feel, think, and respond during challenging discussions.

The physical environment requires careful consideration for high-stakes conversations. Neutral territory helps ensure that neither party feels a psychological disadvantage. When Thomas needed to discuss inheritance plans with his siblings, he chose a private room at their local library rather than any of their homes. This neutral setting helped prevent old family dynamics from overshadowing the critical decisions they needed to make.

The arrangement of space itself communicates intention. Alissa, a family therapist I worked with, discovered that positioning seats at a 45-degree angle rather than directly facing each other reduced confrontational tension while maintaining connection. She also found that having water or tea available did more than provide refreshment—it gave people a natural way to pause and collect their thoughts during intense moments.

Familiar spaces often work better than formal settings for routine conflicts. When Maria needed to address ongoing communication issues with her teenage son, she chose their favorite ice cream shop. The familiar, positive environment helped make a potentially tense conversation feel more approachable. The casual setting allowed for natural breaks in conversation as they ate, preventing the discussion from becoming too intense.

Emotional discussions require particular attention to creating a supportive environment that provides physical and emotional safety. Jennifer, a divorce mediator, transformed her practice by adding elements that actively calmed both parties. She added soft lighting, comfortable seating, and even subtle aromatherapy. Most importantly, she ensured that both parties had easy access to exits and breaks when needed.

Timing considerations proved equally crucial. Rachel eventually had a productive conversation with her daughter by waiting for a quiet Saturday afternoon when they were both relaxed and had plenty of time to talk. They chose to have the discussion while walking in their favorite park—a setting that felt natural and allowed them to be side-by-side rather than face-to-face, reducing tension.

The success of this approach lies in understanding that different conversations require different environments. A discussion about financial concerns might need a private, focused setting with relevant documents at hand. A conversation about relationship dynamics might work better in a more relaxed, informal environment that encourages openness.

Secret #30: Manage Emotions During Tense Moments

Benjamin's hands were shaking as he discussed financial concerns with his wife, Sophia. When he felt his anger rising, he remembered a technique we'd practiced: "Sophia, I need a moment to collect my thoughts. Can we take a five-minute break and then continue?"

This simple pause prevented what could have become a heated argument. When they resumed their conversation, both were calmer and better able to focus on solutions. Benjamin had learned that managing emotions during conflict isn't about suppressing them—it's about acknowledging and channeling them constructively.

Physical techniques provide immediate relief and regulation for intense anger or frustration. Box breathing, a technique borrowed from military training, became Benjamin's go-to tool. By inhaling for four counts, holding for four, exhaling for four, and holding again for four, he could actively engage his parasympathetic nervous system, calming his physiological response to stress.

Progressive muscle relaxation proved particularly effective during seated conversations. Starting with his hands, Benjamin would systematically tense and release each muscle group, releasing physical tension that could otherwise escalate emotional tension. When standing wasn't possible, he found that firmly pressing his feet into the ground helped him feel literally and figuratively grounded.

For those dealing with anxiety or nervousness during difficult conversations, grounding techniques provide a vital anchor to the present moment. Allison, an executive facing a challenging performance review discussion, developed a discrete yet effective approach. When anxiety threatened to overwhelm her, she would engage her senses systematically: naming five things she could see, four she could touch, three she could hear, two she could smell, and one she could taste. This simple practice helped her stay present and focused during crucial conversations.

Another effective grounding technique involves focusing on specific physical sensations. When Thomas felt anxiety rising during family discussions about elder care, he would focus intently on the sensation of his feet touching the ground or his back against the chair. This concrete physical awareness helped prevent his mind from spinning into worst-case scenarios.

For moments of emotional overwhelm, having a structured approach to pausing proved invaluable. Instead of vague requests for time, successful navigators of difficult conversations learned to be specific. "I need five minutes to gather my thoughts" works better than an open-ended break. Moving to a different part of the room can provide both physical and emotional space to reset.

The "empty bowl" meditation, a technique Jennifer learned during our coaching sessions, became her secret weapon during intense negotiations. She would visualize her mind as an empty bowl, allowing thoughts and emotions to flow through without trying to hold onto them. This practice helped her maintain clarity even when discussions became heated.

How to Talk with Friends During Conflict

Friendships present unique challenges when it comes to difficult conversations. Unlike family or professional relationships, friendships are maintained purely by choice, making the stakes of conflict particularly high. Through studying hundreds of friendship dynamics, I've identified approaches that not only preserve these precious bonds during conflict but often strengthen them.

Secret #31: Suggest Solutions That Respect Your Friend's Needs

Madison and Ava's decades-long friendship faced its greatest test when Madison felt increasingly hurt by Ava's chronic lateness. Instead of letting resentment build or making accusations, Madison approached the issue with curiosity and respect.

"Ava, I value our friendship so much, and I want to understand what makes it difficult for you to arrive on time," she began. "Maybe we can find a solution that works for both of us?" This opening created space for a surprising revelation: Ava had been struggling with anxiety that made it increasingly difficult to leave her house. What could have become a friendship-ending conflict instead became an opportunity for deeper understanding and support.

Madison's success came from understanding that effective solutions must consider both parties' needs and constraints. Rather than pushing for her preferred solution—having Ava simply arrive on time—she explored options that acknowledged her friend's challenges while addressing her own need for respect and consideration.

They developed a system that worked for both of them: For important events, Madison would pick Ava up, turning potentially stressful transit time into enjoyable connection time. For casual meet-ups, they built in buffer time and chose locations where arriving at different times wouldn't impact their ability to enjoy each other's company. Most importantly, they established open communication about anxiety levels and timing expectations.

Secret #32: Create Agreements to Grow Your Bond

Lucas and Owen's friendship was tested when a misunderstanding about shared business opportunities threatened to end their 15-year relationship. Instead of letting the friendship fade—as many do when business and personal relationships collide—they decided to use the conflict as a catalyst for growth. Together, they created what they now call their "friendship framework," a thoughtful approach to preventing and handling future challenges.

Their framework began with regular relationship check-ins. Every month, they would meet for coffee specifically to discuss the health of their friendship. These weren't casual catch-ups but structured conversations about what was working well and what needed attention. "It felt awkward at first," Lucas admitted, "but these check-ins helped us catch small issues before they became major problems."

The framework included clear boundaries around business discussions. They designated specific times and places for business conversations, ensuring that their regular friendship time remained protected. When business topics arose naturally, they would acknowledge them but defer detailed discussions to their designated business meetings.

Perhaps most importantly, they developed specific protocols for raising concerns early. Instead of letting discomfort or disagreements simmer, they agreed to use a simple phrase, "I need to check something with you, "to signal that something felt off. This signal helped them address potential issues while they were still manageable.

"It's like creating a user manual for our friendship," Owen explained. "Now we both know how to maintain it." Their approach transformed what could have been a friendship-ending conflict into an opportunity for deeper connection and understanding.

Secret #33: Reassure Your Friend and Show Gratitude

When Zoe and Grace resolved their conflict over wedding planning responsibilities, Zoe ended the conversation with words that transformed their relationship: "Grace, thank you for being willing to have this difficult conversation. Our friendship means the world to me, and I'm grateful we could work through this together."

This moment of genuine gratitude did more than just end the conversation positively—it reinforced their bond and created a foundation for handling future challenges. Zoe understood that how you end a difficult conversation is just as important as how you begin it.

Expressing specific appreciation became a crucial part of her approach. Rather than offering generic thanks, she acknowledged the particular ways Grace had shown up for the conversation: her willingness to listen, her openness to different perspectives, and her patience in working toward solutions. This specificity helped Grace feel truly seen and valued.

Acknowledging shared effort proved equally important. By recognizing that both parties had worked to find a resolution, Zoe reinforced their partnership in maintaining the friendship. "We both showed up ready to understand each other," she noted, "and that's what made this conversation successful."

Looking forward positively became the final piece of their reconciliation. Instead of dwelling on the conflict they'd resolved, Zoe focused on the future they would share: "I'm excited to continue planning this wedding together, knowing we can handle challenges when they arise."

How to Navigate Conflict at the Workplace

Professional environments present unique challenges when it comes to handling difficult conversations. The stakes often involve careers, reputations, and team dynamics. Through my extensive work with organizations, I've found that successful workplace conflict resolution requires a delicate balance of assertiveness and diplomacy, combined with clear communication techniques that maintain professional relationships.

Secret #34: Use "I" Statements to Address Issues Clearly and Respectfully

Adrian, a project manager, transformed a tense team situation with a simple shift in language. Instead of saying, "You never meet deadlines," he said, "I feel concerned when deliverables are delayed because it impacts the entire team's ability to succeed."

This subtle change in language had a profound effect. By focusing on impact rather than blame, Adrian opened the door for collaborative problem-solving. Instead of becoming defensive, his team member felt comfortable sharing the challenges he faced with workload management.

For performance issues, Adrian developed a systematic approach using what he called the "observation-impact-inquiry-solution" framework. When noticing project timelines extending, he would share his observation directly but without judgment: "I notice our project timelines are extending beyond our initial estimates." He would then express his concern about the impact: "I'm concerned about meeting our quarterly goals."

The next step in Adrian's framework involved collaborative inquiry: "I wonder if we could explore what's causing the delays?" This approach invited joint problem-solving rather than accusation. Finally, he would suggest a path forward: "I suggest we review our process together to identify where we might need additional support or resources."

When addressing behavioral concerns, Adrian developed an extended approach that connected emotions, situations, and outcomes. During a period when late-starting meetings were affecting team productivity, he framed the issue this way: "I feel frustrated when our meetings start late because it impacts our team's productivity. I need us to commit to starting on time so we can make the most of everyone's time." This approach acknowledged his emotional response while focusing on the practical impact and desired outcome.

Adrian found that expressing appreciation before concerns helped maintain positive connections for relationship dynamics. When addressing communication issues with a remote team member, he might say: "I value our working relationship. I feel disconnected when we only communicate through email because I miss our direct interactions. I hope we can schedule regular check-ins." This framework helped preserve relationships while addressing important issues.

Secret #35: Understand Perspectives Through Careful Listening

Camilla, a department head at a tech company, earned a reputation for her exceptional ability to resolve team conflicts. Her secret was what she called "360-degree listening," a comprehensive approach to understanding not just words but emotions, context, and underlying needs.

Camilla masterfully demonstrated this approach during a particularly heated disagreement between two team members over project priorities. Instead of jumping to solutions, she created space for each person to share their perspective fully. Her active listening techniques included paraphrasing key points to ensure understanding: "Let me make sure I'm following—you're concerned about the timeline because...?"

When emotions ran high, she would acknowledge them directly while maintaining professional boundaries: "I can hear how passionate you both are about getting this right." This validation often helped team members feel heard enough to move toward solutions.

Her body language played a crucial role in creating a safe space for sharing. She maintained an open posture, made appropriate eye contact, and used subtle nodding to show engagement. Perhaps most importantly, she learned to match her energy level to the situation—calm and steady during tense moments, energetic and encouraging when building momentum toward solutions.

Secret #36: Respond Wisely, Not Aggressively, to Workplace Disrespect

When Marcus, a senior developer, found himself being publicly criticized in a cross-team meeting, his first instinct was to defend himself aggressively. Instead, drawing on techniques we'd practiced, he transformed an inflammatory situation into an opportunity for mutual understanding.

"I felt attacked and disrespected," Marcus shared later. "But I remembered that aggressive responses only escalate conflicts.

Instead of firing back, I chose to respond with professionalism and wisdom." His approach became a model for handling workplace conflicts constructively.

Marcus began by maintaining his composure through deliberate breathing exercises. While his colleague continued criticizing his team's approach, Marcus focused on taking slow, deep breaths, keeping his body language calm and professional. This physical self-regulation helped him maintain emotional balance.

When he did respond, Marcus acknowledged his colleague's concerns without accepting unfair criticism: "I appreciate you raising these concerns about our approach. I'd like to share some context about our decision-making process that might help clarify things." By focusing on facts rather than emotions, he kept the discussion professional.

Rather than engaging in a public debate, Marcus suggested a more appropriate forum: "These are important points you're raising. Could we schedule time this afternoon to discuss them in detail? I want to ensure we can give this the attention it deserves." This approach demonstrated respect for both the concerns raised and the broader team's time.

The resolution process that followed became a template for handling similar situations. Marcus and his colleague met privately, where they could explore concerns more openly. They discovered that the conflict stemmed largely from miscommunication about project constraints and priorities. By seeking to understand underlying concerns rather than defending positions, they found common ground that led to improved collaboration.

Moving Forward: Implementing These Approaches

As we conclude this exploration of difficult conversations, remember that mastering these skills requires practice and patience. Start with one technique that resonates most strongly with you. Perhaps it's using "and" instead of "but" in challenging discussions or practicing emotional regulation techniques during stressful situations.

Consider keeping a conversation journal to track your progress. Note which approaches work best in different situations and how people respond to various techniques. Pay attention to your own emotional patterns and triggers, using this awareness to prepare for future challenging conversations.

Remember that every difficult conversation is an opportunity —not just to resolve immediate issues but to strengthen relationships and build trust. When handled skillfully, these moments can transform potential conflicts into deeper connections and understanding.

In the next chapter, we'll explore how to use storytelling to enhance your charisma and connection with others. The skills you've learned here—emotional awareness, careful word choice, and respectful engagement—will serve as a foundation for crafting and sharing stories that resonate deeply with others.

The journey to mastering difficult conversations is ongoing, but with these techniques as your guide, you're well-equipped to transform challenging moments into opportunities for growth and connection.

Key Takeaways

- Acknowledge conflicts openly and early.
- Choose appropriate timing and settings for difficult conversations.
- Manage emotions actively during tense moments.
- Suggest solutions with respect and flexibility.
- Create clear agreements that strengthen relationships.
- Show genuine gratitude and reassurance.
- Use "I" statements to maintain respect.
- Listen carefully to understand all perspectives.
- Build solutions collaboratively.

Action Steps

1. Practice crafting "I" statements for a current challenge.
2. Set up a proper time and place for an overdue difficult conversation.
3. Create a personal emotional management plan.
4. Develop a framework for agreements with important relationships.
5. Practice active listening in your next conflict situation.
6. Write appreciation statements to use after difficult conversations.
7. Design a collaborative solution process for a current conflict.

Chapter 5
How to Use Storytelling to Be Charismatic

The room was silent except for the gentle hum of the air conditioning. Thirty executives sat motionless, their eyes fixed on Hannah, a junior analyst presenting her findings about a potential market expansion. But unlike the countless data-heavy presentations they'd seen before, this one was different. Hannah began not with charts or graphs but with a story:

"Last month, I watched my grandmother try to order groceries online for the first time. Her fingers trembled as she navigated the website, her frustration mounting with each click. 'Why can't this be simpler?' she asked. That moment transformed how I saw our market expansion opportunity. Today, I'm not just sharing data about an aging population—I'm sharing a vision of how we can make technology more accessible for people like my grandmother."

By the end of her presentation, Hannah had secured full funding for her proposal. The power of her success wasn't just in the data—it was in her ability to weave that data into a story that resonated with everyone in the room.

Why Storytelling Matters

In my years of studying human communication, I've discovered that stories are far more than entertainment—they're the fundamental building blocks of human connection and understanding. When we share stories, we're not just exchanging information; we're creating shared experiences that bridge gaps in understanding and forge emotional bonds. The best communicators I've worked with don't just tell stories—they craft experiences that transform perspectives and inspire action.

Secret #37: Stories Create Emotional Bonds

Oliver's transformation from a competent but overlooked middle manager to his company's most influential leader began with a simple realization: Facts inform, but stories transform.

"I used to overwhelm my team with data and directives," he told me during one of our coaching sessions. "Then I started sharing stories about why our work mattered." He recounted how his approach to announcing a major policy change shifted dramatically. Where he once would have said, "Our customer satisfaction scores have dropped 12% in the last quarter. We need to implement new response time standards," he instead shared a powerful narrative:

"Last week, I spoke with Maria, a customer who missed her daughter's graduation because our service failure left her stranded. Her story haunts me, and I know we can do better.

Let me share what happened, and then let's talk about how we can ensure it never happens again."

The difference in his team's response was immediate and profound. Instead of grudging compliance, he got passionate engagement. Oliver had discovered what master communicators have always known: stories create emotional resonance that facts alone never can.

Through our work together, Oliver developed what he calls his "story structure framework," a fluid approach that begins by grounding each story in a specific moment. He learned to share not just what happened but also his genuine emotions and thoughts during that moment. Most importantly, he discovered how to connect his experiences to universal themes that everyone could relate to. Finally, he would thoughtfully bridge from the story to the larger message he wanted to convey.

The transformation in his team's engagement was remarkable. "People stopped checking their phones during meetings," he noted. "Instead, they were leaning in, asking questions, and sharing their own stories. That's when I knew we'd created a real connection."

The key to Oliver's success lie in his attention to detail. Rather than speaking in generalities, he painted vivid pictures with his words. When he described Maria's missed graduation, he included the small details that made the story come alive—the way her voice cracked when she mentioned her daughter's name, the graduation card she'd planned to hand-deliver, the celebratory dinner reservation that went unused. These specifics transformed a simple customer service story into a powerful reminder of why their work mattered.

Secret #38: Stories Simplify Complex Ideas

Charlotte, a quantum physicist, faced a common challenge: explaining her research to non-scientists. Her breakthrough came when she stopped trying to explain quantum entanglement with equations and instead told this story:

"Imagine you have two dancers who have practiced together for years. Even when they're separated by an entire stage, they move in perfect synchronization—when one spins, the other spins, when one leaps, the other leaps, instantly and mysteriously connected. That's similar to what happens with entangled particles."

This simple metaphor accomplished what pages of technical explanations couldn't—it made a complex concept accessible and memorable. Charlotte's success led her to develop a systematic approach to transforming technical concepts into engaging narratives.

Her journey to storytelling mastery began with a fundamental insight: Every technical concept, no matter how abstract, has a human element. She started by asking herself three essential questions about each research topic: *Who would be affected by this discovery? What difference could it make in people's lives? Why should anyone outside her field care about these findings?*

The search for perfect analogies became an iterative process of discovery. The quantum entanglement dancers weren't her first attempt at explanation—she'd also tried comparing them to synchronized swimmers, mirror images, and even identical twins. But she found that dance resonated most deeply with people, perhaps because it combined art and precision in a way that paralleled her scientific work.

Testing became a crucial part of her storytelling development. She would try out her analogies on diverse audiences, from her teenage nephew to her elderly neighbor. Each conversation provided valuable insights. When her mother asked, "But how do the dancers know when to move?" Charlotte realized she needed to emphasize the mysterious, instantaneous nature of quantum entanglement more clearly. When a colleague pointed out that dancers sometimes make mistakes while quantum entanglement is perfect, she adapted her story to address this limitation.

Through this process of continuous refinement, Charlotte developed what she calls her "story sensors," an intuitive ability to read audience reactions and adjust her explanations in real time. She learned to watch for furrowed brows, shifting postures, and other subtle signs of confusion or engagement. Most importantly, she discovered that the best analogies aren't just accurate—they're memorable and engaging enough to be retold.

Elements of a Captivating Story

The difference between a story that captivates and one that falls flat often lies in its structural elements. I've identified key components that consistently create memorable narratives by studying thousands of presentations, conversations, and speeches. When these elements are thoughtfully crafted and skillfully combined, they create stories that don't just engage —they transform.

Secret #39: Start With a Hook

Maya's presentation about sustainable energy was scheduled for 4:30 p.m.—the dreaded post-lunch, end-of-day slot when attention spans are at their lowest. Instead of beginning with traditional pleasantries, she opened with:

"Three months ago, in a remote village in India, a twelve-year-old girl read her first book after sunset. Not by candlelight or kerosene lamp, but by a solar-powered LED light that costs less than a cup of coffee. Today, I want to show you how we can bring that same transformation to millions more."

The room was instantly energized. Maya had mastered what I call the "first seven seconds rule," the crucial moment when you either capture or lose your audience's attention.

Through our work together, Maya developed what she calls her "hook library," a collection of opening techniques that reliably grab attention and create emotional investment. She discovered that surprising statistics could jolt an audience out of complacency, but only if they were immediately followed by a human context that made those numbers meaningful. Personal stories proved powerful, but they needed to be carefully chosen to resonate with the specific audience's experiences and aspirations.

The art of building anticipation became one of Maya's signature skills. She learned to structure her openings like skilled novelists structure their first pages—providing enough intrigue to create questions in the audience's minds while holding back enough information to maintain curiosity. "Think of it like a movie trailer," she would say. "You want to promise something compelling without giving away the whole story."

Secret #40: Build a Relatable Conflict

Andrew, a sales trainer, noticed his workshops on handling

customer objections weren't resonating until he restructured them around a story from his own early career:

"Picture this: My first big sales presentation, my dream client, and right as I'm building to my close, the CFO interrupts with the one objection I hadn't prepared for. My palms start sweating, my mouth goes dry, and in that moment, I learn the most valuable lesson of my career..."

By sharing his own moment of tension and vulnerability, Andrew created what master storytellers call a "conflict bridge," a situation so relatable that listeners can't help but invest emotionally in the outcome. The power of this approach lay not just in the conflict itself but in how Andrew crafted and delivered it.

He learned to make conflicts real by grounding them in authentic situations that his audience could picture themselves experiencing. Rather than presenting himself as a flawless expert, he shared genuine moments of struggle and uncertainty. "When I describe my hands shaking during that presentation," he explained, "every sales professional in the room knows exactly how that feels. They're not just hearing my story—they're reliving their own moments of pressure."

The art of keeping stakes relatable became one of Andrew's key insights. While dramatic stories of million-dollar deals gone wrong might seem exciting, he found that his audiences connected more deeply with situations that mirrored their daily challenges. A story about fumbling with technology during a client call or blanking on a key detail during a presentation often resonated more than tales of grand successes or failures.

Building tension naturally emerged as another crucial skill. Andrew developed what he calls the "tension ladder," a way of layering challenges that mirrors how pressure builds in real situations. Instead of rushing to the main conflict, he learned to show how small complications can compound into significant challenges. This approach helped his audience see how seemingly minor issues could escalate into major problems if not handled skillfully.

Speaking With Charisma

Charisma isn't just about natural charm or magnetic personality—it's about creating meaningful connections through intentional communication. The most charismatic speakers I've worked with understand that their power lies not in their own performance but in their ability to make others feel seen, understood, and inspired. Through storytelling, they transform ordinary messages into extraordinary moments of connection.

Secret #41: Align Stories with Your Message

"The story was great, but what was the point?" This feedback from a colleague transformed how Sophia approached storytelling in her role as a team leader. She realized that entertaining stories without a clear purpose were like beautiful wrapping paper with no gift inside.

Sophia's journey to mastering story-message alignment began with that crucial piece of feedback about her purposeless stories. In our work together, she developed what she calls her "message-first framework." Before selecting or crafting any story, she would first achieve absolute clarity about her core message. "I started asking myself: *What do I want my audience to think, feel, and do differently after hearing this?*" she explained.

The framework evolved into a natural flow that felt more like a conversation than a presentation. She discovered that the transition between the story and the message was as crucial as the story itself. These bridges, as she called them, needed to feel organic while still guiding listeners to the intended conclusion. She practiced creating these transitions until they became seamless: "Just as Maria learned to trust her instincts in that crucial moment, we need to trust our experience when making decisions about..."

The real breakthrough came when Sophia started thinking of stories as illumination rather than illustration. Instead of using stories to merely demonstrate her points, she chose stories that shed new light on her message, helping her audience see familiar concepts from fresh angles. This shift transformed her presentations from informative to inspiring.

"Every story needs to earn its place" became her mantra. She developed a rigorous evaluation process for each potential story, asking herself: *Does this story deepen understanding of the core message? Does it create an emotional connection that makes the message more compelling? Does it make abstract concepts concrete and actionable?* Stories that couldn't meet these criteria, no matter how entertaining, were set aside for other contexts.

Secret #42: Make Your Listener the Hero

When James, a career coach, worked with clients, he noticed a pattern: The more he made his advice about their story rather than his, the more engaged and motivated they became. His transformation began when he realized that his impressive collection of success stories about past clients wasn't having the impact he'd hoped for.

"I had all these great stories about people overcoming career challenges," he explained during one of our coaching sessions. "But I noticed my clients would listen politely, nod, and then say something like, 'That's great for them, but my situation is different.'" The breakthrough came when he shifted from telling success stories about his past clients to helping current clients envision their own success stories.

Instead of saying, "Let me tell you about someone else who overcame this challenge," he began with, "Imagine yourself six months from now, walking into that corner office..." This simple shift transformed his practice. He tapped into a powerful source of motivation and engagement by making his clients the protagonists of their own future stories.

James developed what he calls "future story mapping," a technique for helping people craft compelling narratives about their potential. He would guide clients through a structured visualization process, helping them imagine not just the end goal but the journey toward it. "When we create a detailed story about overcoming obstacles and achieving goals," he explained, "we're actually rehearsing success mentally. It makes the path forward feel both real and achievable."

The technique proved particularly powerful when helping clients prepare for job interviews. Rather than just coaching them on answer techniques, he would help them craft their professional narrative—a story that connected their past experiences, present ambitions, and future potential. "Once someone can tell a compelling story about their career journey," he noted, "interview questions become opportunities to share chapters of that larger narrative."

This approach transformed how his clients viewed challenges. Instead of seeing obstacles as potential failure points, they began to view them as plot points in their success story. "Every hero's journey has obstacles," James would remind them. "What matters is how you choose to engage with them."

The next time you share a story, remember that your listener isn't just an audience member—they're a potential hero waiting to see themselves in your narrative. By making space for their experience and perspective, you transform your story from a monologue into a shared journey of discovery and growth.

Moving Forward: Building Your Storytelling Practice

The journey to becoming a masterful storyteller begins with understanding that every interaction is an opportunity to practice and refine your skills. Start by collecting stories that illustrate your core messages—moments from your own experience that carry universal lessons or insights. These don't need to be dramatic or life-changing events; the most relatable stories often come from everyday experiences that reveal more profound truths.

Develop your ability to simplify complex ideas through analogy and metaphor. Practice explaining challenging concepts to people outside your field, paying attention to which comparisons resonate and which fall flat. Remember Charlotte's iterative approach to developing her quantum entanglement story—each attempt at explanation is an opportunity to refine your technique.

Create a collection of strong opening hooks for different situations. Like Maya, experiment with various approaches—

surprising statistics, vivid scenes, and thought-provoking questions. Pay attention to which openings capture attention most effectively with different audiences.

Most importantly, focus on making your stories interactive rather than performative. Create spaces within your narratives where listeners can insert their own experiences and insights. Remember James's shift from telling success stories to helping clients envision their own—the most powerful stories are those that involve your audience as active participants rather than passive listeners.

Practice these techniques in low-stakes situations before applying them to important presentations or meetings. Share stories with friends, family, or trusted colleagues and ask for specific feedback about which elements resonated most strongly and which could be refined.

Remember that the goal isn't to become a polished performer but to develop authentic ways of connecting with others through shared narratives. Your unique experiences and perspectives are valuable—the key is learning to share them in ways that create meaningful connections and inspire positive change.

In the next chapter, we'll explore how to adapt your communication style to different personalities and situations. The storytelling techniques you've learned here will serve as powerful tools for connecting with diverse audiences and making your message memorable across various contexts.

Key Takeaways

- Stories create emotional connections that facts alone cannot achieve.
- Well-crafted stories can simplify complex ideas.
- A strong hook captures attention instantly.
- Relatable conflict keeps listeners engaged.
- Stories must align with and reinforce your message.
- Making the listener the hero increases engagement.

Action Steps

1. Write down three personal stories that could illustrate your core messages.
2. Practice telling a complex idea through a simple analogy.
3. Create three different hooks for your next important presentation.
4. Record yourself telling a story and analyze your delivery.
5. Ask a friend to help you practice making stories more interactive.
6. Build your story library with different types of anecdotes for various situations.

Chapter 6
How to Make People Like You

Rebecca stood at the edge of the conference room, taking in the scene before her. In one corner, C-suite executives discussed quarterly projections in crisp, data-driven language. Near the coffee station, creative team members shared ideas with animated gestures and enthusiastic expressions. By the whiteboard, engineers debated technical specifications with precise terminology and measured tones.

As the new Chief of Innovation, Rebecca needed to connect with all of them. But more importantly, she needed them to connect with each other. What happened next would become a masterclass in adaptability that I still share in my workshops today.

Reading the Room

The ability to read and adapt to different social environments is perhaps the most underrated skill in communication. It's not about changing who you are—it's about presenting the most appropriate version of yourself for each context. In studying hundreds of successful leaders and communicators, I've discovered that those who excel at building connections across different groups share a common trait: They're like social chameleons, able to blend seamlessly into any environment while maintaining their authentic core.

This adaptability isn't about being inauthentic or manipulative. Instead, it's about understanding that different contexts require different aspects of our personality to shine through. Just as we naturally speak differently to a child than we do to a colleague, skilled communicators adjust their approach based on their audience while remaining true to their fundamental values and character.

Secret #43: Observe Before You Engage

Marcus's transformation from awkward newcomer to trusted team leader began with a simple practice: observation. "I used to barrel into conversations, eager to prove myself," he told me during one of our coaching sessions. "Then, I learned the power of watching and listening first."

At his first executive leadership summit, instead of immediately joining discussions, Marcus spent the first 30 minutes observing the dynamics of different conversation groups. He noticed how the CFO used precise numbers in her speech while the Creative Director spoke in metaphors and visual descriptions. He picked up on how some groups stood in tight circles while others maintained more open formations that welcomed newcomers.

The insights he gained during those 30 minutes proved invaluable. When he finally approached a group discussing digital transformation—his area of expertise—he didn't immediately launch into sharing his knowledge. Instead, he first observed their conversation pattern, noting how they took turns building on each other's ideas rather than competing for airtime. When he did join in, he matched this collaborative style, adding his insights in a way that complemented rather than interrupted the existing flow.

Through repeated practice, Marcus developed what we now call the "three-level observation" technique. The first level focused on energy dynamics—reading the overall mood and animation level of different groups. Was the discussion intense and focused, or relaxed and exploratory? Were people leaning in with enthusiasm or maintaining professional distance?

The second level examined conversation styles. Marcus learned to notice not just what people were saying but how they were saying it. Were they using formal business language or casual expressions? Did they prefer direct statements or exploratory questions? Understanding these patterns helped him adjust his own communication style to match.

The third level involved looking for opening signals—those subtle invitations that suggest a group is open to new participants. These might be physical cues, like slight shifts in standing positions to create space for others or conversational pauses that offered natural entry points.

Secret #44: Tailor Your Approach to the Group Based on Observation

Naomi's role as a global consultant required her to switch between vastly different professional cultures, often multiple times in the same day. One morning, she might be in a formal board meeting with traditional executives, and that afternoon, she could find herself brainstorming with a startup team in a converted warehouse.

Her success came from understanding that each environment had its own conversational ecosystem. In the boardroom, she would use precise language, maintain direct eye contact, and structure her thoughts in clear, linear progressions. The same afternoon, working with the startup team, she would adopt a more collaborative tone, embrace industry-specific casual language, and engage in more spontaneous idea generation.

"It's like having a conversational wardrobe," Naomi explained during one of our coaching sessions. "Just as you wouldn't wear a formal suit to a beach party, you shouldn't use board-room language in a casual brainstorming session." This insight transformed how she prepared for each interaction.

The key to her adaptability lay in her preparation routine. Before any meeting, Naomi would ask herself three crucial questions: *What's the expected level of formality in this environment? What language and terms are common among these people? What communication style will help others feel most comfortable and engaged?*

Over time, Naomi developed what she called her "cultural compass," an internal guide for navigating different professional environments. In traditional corporate settings, she learned that credibility often came from demonstrating expertise through well-structured presentations and data-backed assertions. In creative agencies, she found that authenticity and originality carried more weight than formal credentials.

Flexibility in Communication Styles

The most successful communicators understand that genuine connection requires more than just speaking clearly—it requires speaking in a way that resonates with each specific audience. Through years of observation and research, I've discovered that mastering this flexibility while maintaining authenticity is both an art and a science.

Secret #45: Embrace the Platinum Rule

We're all familiar with the Golden Rule: Treat others as you would want to be treated. But in communication, I've found that the Platinum Rule is even more powerful: Treat others as they want to be treated. This insight transformed how Anthony approached his role as a project manager.

"I used to get frustrated when team members didn't respond to my communication style," Anthony shared during one of our sessions. "I love detailed emails with bullet points and clear action items. But I noticed some team members rarely read my emails thoroughly, while others wanted even more detail than I provided."

His breakthrough came when he started asking each team member about their preferred communication style. The insights he gained were revelatory. Jasmine, his technical lead, preferred brief voice messages that she could listen to while coding. James, the marketing director, wanted in-person check-ins where he could sketch ideas on a whiteboard. Tori, the data analyst, appreciated Anthony's detailed emails but wanted them scheduled for her early morning review time when she was freshest.

Through careful observation and direct feedback, Anthony developed a sophisticated understanding of different information processing styles. He noticed that visual learners often requested written documentation and responded well to diagrams and charts. Auditory learners preferred verbal updates and often processed information better through discussion. Interactive learners needed to engage with ideas through conversation and hands-on experience.

Timing preferences emerged as another crucial factor. Early morning readers like Tori wanted detailed information they could process before the day's interruptions began. Mid-day meeting participants often preferred shorter, more focused interactions. End-of-day summarizers needed wrap-up communications that helped them organize their thoughts and plan for the next day.

Secret #46: Master the Art of Code-Switching

Dr. Amara Chen's research in sociolinguistics took on new meaning when she became a department head at a major university. Suddenly, she wasn't just studying code-switching —the ability to alternate between different communication styles—she was living it. Her typical day became a masterclass in adaptive communication.

"In one day, I might present research to fellow academics, explain complex concepts to undergraduate students, discuss budgets with administrators, and chat with maintenance staff about building issues," she explained during our interview. "Each interaction required a different vocabulary, pace, and style."

Through careful practice and reflection, Dr. Chen developed what she calls "communication presets," not rigid scripts but flexible frameworks for different contexts. With fellow researchers, she would employ technical terminology and academic references, knowing this precision was essential for scholarly discourse. When working with students, she transformed complex theories into relatable analogies and real-world examples. In administrative meetings, she focused on concrete outcomes and metrics that resonated with decision-makers.

The key to her success lay not in merely switching vocabulary but in understanding the underlying thought patterns and priorities of each group. She noticed that academics valued theoretical depth, students responded to practical applications, and administrators needed clear connections to institutional goals.

"Code-switching isn't about being fake," she emphasized during one of our discussions. "It's about creating bridges of understanding while staying true to yourself." She demonstrated this authenticity by maintaining her passionate interest in her field across all contexts, just expressing it in ways that connected most effectively with each audience.

Engaging With Diverse Personalities

In today's interconnected world, the ability to engage effectively with diverse personalities isn't just nice to have—it's essential for success. Through studying successful communicators across cultures and industries, I've discovered that the most effective approaches focus on finding connection points while respecting and celebrating differences.

Secret #47: Find Common Ground Across Differences

Jason's role as an international business consultant taught him that finding common ground requires more than just identifying shared interests—it requires genuine curiosity about others' perspectives. During a particularly challenging merger between Japanese and American companies, he transformed potential culture clashes into opportunities for connection.

"Instead of focusing on differences in communication styles, I started asking questions about shared experiences," Jason explained. "Both teams had stories about their children's school activities, their morning commutes, their favorite lunch spots. These universal experiences became bridges."

He developed a technique he calls "universal entry points," topics that resonated across cultural boundaries. Food proved to be a particularly effective starting point; discussions about local cuisines often led to deeper conversations about traditions and values. Family experiences, while approached differently across cultures, provided another rich source of connection. Personal growth and professional challenges, he discovered, were universal themes that transcended cultural differences.

The power of Jason's approach lies not just in the topics he chose but also in how he approached them. Rather than using these conversations as mere ice-breakers, he showed genuine curiosity about how different cultures approached common life experiences. This authentic interest helped others feel valued and understood, creating a foundation for deeper professional relationships.

Secret #48: Stay Calm Amid Contrasting Opinions

Maria's experience as a diplomatic liaison taught her that the most powerful tool in handling disagreements isn't clever argumentation—it's emotional stability. During a heated international negotiation, she demonstrated this principle in a way that transformed not just the immediate situation but her entire team's approach to conflict.

When strongly opposing views emerged about a proposed initiative, Maria maintained her composure and used neutral language to acknowledge each perspective. "I noticed that the more heated others became, the more important it was for me to remain calm and curious," she shared. "It was like being in the eye of a storm—the calmer I stayed, the more others began to moderate their own responses."

This observation led to what I now call "the stability spiral." As tensions rise, deliberately increase your own steadiness. Maria developed specific techniques for maintaining this stability. She would consciously slow her speaking pace, using the extra moments to choose words carefully. Her tone would become softer, not in volume but in emotional intensity. Even her gestures would become more measured and deliberate.

The physical aspects of this approach proved as vital as the verbal ones. Maria learned to maintain an open posture even when others became defensive. She would keep her breathing steady and deep, understanding that physiological calm promotes mental clarity. These subtle physical cues often had a ripple effect, unconsciously influencing others to mirror her composure.

Secret #49: Bring People Together

When Raj took over as director of a diverse and previously divided department, he saw his role not just as a leader but as a connector. His insight that "many conflicts stemmed from people simply not knowing each other as humans" led to a revolutionary approach to team building.

Instead of focusing on formal team-building exercises, Raj created what he called "connection points," organic opportunities for meaningful interaction between people who might not naturally cross paths. He redesigned project teams to bring together people from different backgrounds and specialties. Lunch groups were thoughtfully organized to mix departments and hierarchical levels. Informal skill-sharing sessions allowed people to teach others about their expertise or interests.

But perhaps his most innovative technique was what he called "spotlight connections," moments where he would highlight complementary skills or shared interests between team members who might not otherwise interact. During meetings, he would make connections like, "Arlow, your experience with urban photography might offer an interesting perspective on the visual branding challenge that Ted is working on." These seemingly casual observations often led to productive collaborations.

Raj's approach went beyond simple networking. He created a "connection map" of his department, regularly identifying potential synergies between different teams and individuals. When he noticed complementary skills or interests, he would create natural opportunities for those people to work together or share ideas.

Secret #50: Use Humor to Break Barriers

Claire's success as a global team leader came in part from her skillful use of humor to bridge cultural and professional gaps. However, her approach to humor was anything but casual—it was carefully considered and situationally aware.

"I learned that humor isn't just about making people laugh—it's about creating shared moments of joy," she explained. Through careful observation and occasional missteps, she developed what she calls "safe humor zones," topics and styles that could bring people together without risking offense or misunderstanding.

Claire found that universal experiences provided the safest and most effective source of humor. Comments about the challenges of Monday mornings or the strength of office coffee resonated across cultural boundaries. Weather-related observations, technology mishaps, and gentle self-deprecating humor about common workplace situations proved consistently effective.

More importantly, she learned when not to use humor. She avoided sarcasm entirely, recognizing that it could be misinterpreted across cultures. She steered clear of humor that might make anyone feel excluded or required specific cultural knowledge to understand. Personal appearances, individual characteristics, and cultural differences were strictly off-limits.

Her most valuable skill was reading the room's receptiveness to humor. In some situations, a gentle smile or warmly shared observation was sufficient. In others, particularly after building trust with a group, she might share funny stories about her own professional mishaps, always ensuring the story's lesson or insight was clear.

Moving Forward: Implementing Adaptability in Your Communication

As we conclude this exploration of adaptability in communication, remember that the goal isn't to become a different person for each situation—it's about developing the flexibility to connect authentically with diverse audiences while maintaining your core identity.

Begin by practicing the three-level observation technique in low-stakes social situations. Notice the energy dynamics, conversation patterns, and opening signals in different groups. Pay attention to how successful communicators adapt their style while maintaining authenticity.

Develop your own set of communication presets for different contexts. Think about the various professional and social environments you encounter regularly. What adjustments in language, tone, and style might help you connect more effectively in each situation?

Most importantly, maintain curiosity about different communication styles and preferences. Ask colleagues about their preferred ways of receiving information. Notice what makes different people feel heard and understood. Use this knowledge to build bridges across different personality types and communication styles.

Remember, adaptability in communication isn't about manipulation—it's about creating understanding and connection. When you learn to adapt your communication style thoughtfully and authentically, you create opportunities for deeper, more meaningful interactions with people from all walks of life.

In the next chapter, we'll explore how these adaptability skills can be applied specifically to professional settings, helping you navigate complex workplace dynamics with confidence and grace.

Key Takeaways

- Observation is the foundation of effective adaptability.
- Different environments require different communication approaches.
- The Platinum Rule surpasses the Golden Rule in communication.
- Code-switching is about building bridges while maintaining authenticity.
- Common ground exists even across significant differences.
- Calm stability is crucial during disagreements.
- Connection-building elevates your value in any group.
- Appropriate humor can break down barriers when used wisely.

Action Steps

1. Practice the three-level observation technique in low-stakes social situations.
2. Create a list of your own communication presets for different contexts.
3. Ask five colleagues about their preferred communication styles.

4. Identify three universal topics you can use to build connections.
5. Practice maintaining calm during challenging conversations.
6. Look for opportunities to connect others with shared interests.
7. Develop a repertoire of safe, appropriate humor for different settings.
8. Record yourself in different social contexts to observe your adaptation style.

Chapter 7
How to Influence Others
Without Pressure

The conference room fell silent as Katherine finished her presentation. Just six months ago, this same executive board had flatly rejected her proposal for a company-wide sustainability initiative. But today was different. As she watched the CEO nod approvingly, she knew her approach had succeeded—not because she had pushed harder, but because she had learned to inspire rather than insist.

"What changed?" I asked her later. "I stopped trying to win an argument," she explained, "and started building a shared vision. The difference was transformative."

Katherine's journey from frustrated advocate to influential leader illustrates a fundamental truth about persuasion: Real influence doesn't come from pressure or manipulation—it comes from creating genuine connection and shared understanding.

The Foundations of Persuasion

Before you can influence others effectively, you must establish a foundation of trust and understanding. Through years of studying successful change agents across industries, I've discovered that the most persuasive people focus first on building relationships and understanding perspectives before attempting to change minds.

Secret #51: Build Credibility First

Michael's story perfectly illustrates the power of earned credibility. As a new sustainability consultant, he was eager to transform his clients' operations. But his early attempts at persuasion fell flat despite his impressive expertise and passionate presentations. The breakthrough came through an unexpected realization about the nature of trust.

Instead of leading with grand proposals for organizational transformation, Michael began focusing on small, immediately implementable changes. For one manufacturing client, he identified three simple energy-saving modifications that would show measurable results within a month: LED lighting upgrades in high-use areas, automated thermostat programming, and leak detection in compressed air systems.

The impact of this approach extended far beyond the initial energy savings. Each small success built credibility for larger proposals, creating what Michael called a "trust cascade." He discovered that demonstrating expertise through action carried far more weight than simply claiming it on paper. His meticulous documentation of results and transparent communication about both successes and limitations transformed his relationship with clients.

"When I started acknowledging what wouldn't work as readily as what would," he explained during one of our sessions, "clients began trusting my judgment more deeply." He found that sharing uncertainties and providing regular progress updates actually strengthened his credibility rather than undermining it. This transparent approach transformed him from an outside consultant pushing for change into a trusted advisor guiding sustainable progress.

The key to Michael's success was his understanding that credibility isn't claimed—it's earned through consistent demonstration of value and honesty. By starting with easily verifiable solutions and building upon each successful implementation, he created a foundation of trust that made more significant changes possible.

Secret #52: Understand Their Perspective

Amanda's role as a change management consultant taught her that perspective-taking isn't just about empathy—it's about gathering intelligence crucial for effective persuasion. Her breakthrough project involved helping a traditional manufacturing company adopt new digital technologies, a challenge that initially seemed insurmountable given the resistance she encountered.

"Instead of presenting the benefits of digital transformation immediately," she shared during our discussion, "I spent the first two weeks just listening." She conducted what she calls "perspective interviews," focusing first on understanding the current state of operations and employee experiences. Through careful questioning, she discovered that many employees took genuine pride in their traditional manufacturing processes and worried that digitalization might devalue their hard-earned expertise.

Amanda developed a systematic approach to these interviews, starting with questions about what worked well in the current system. "Tell me about your best day at work," she would ask, or "What parts of your job make you most proud?" These questions revealed valuable insights about the company's strengths that she could later incorporate into her proposals.

Next, she explored challenges, but with a crucial twist. Instead of asking directly about problems, she would inquire about what kept people up at night or what they wished they could do better. This approach often revealed deeper concerns than surface-level complaints. One supervisor shared how he worried about losing his team's respect if he couldn't help them navigate the new systems effectively.

Then, she turned her attention to their vision for the future. Through thoughtful questions about their ideal workday and how technology could make their jobs easier, she uncovered not just their surface-level concerns about digitalization but their deeper hopes and fears about workplace change. She discovered that many employees weren't resistant to technology itself—they were afraid of being left behind or becoming obsolete.

This investment in understanding paid off dramatically. When Amanda finally presented her proposal, she could directly address concerns before they were raised and highlight benefits that resonated with each department's specific needs. "The key," she explained, "was that I wasn't selling a solution anymore—I was addressing needs they'd already expressed to me."

Her final presentation incorporated specific examples from her interviews, showing how the proposed changes would enhance rather than replace valued skills. She demonstrated how digital tools could help experienced workers share their knowledge more effectively with newcomers, turning their expertise into a lasting legacy.

Crafting a Compelling Argument

The art of persuasion lies not just in what you say but in how you present your ideas. Through studying countless successful and failed attempts at influence, I've identified key elements that transform ordinary arguments into compelling visions for change.

Secret #53: Use Stories to Connect

Ryan's campaign to revamp his company's customer service protocols was stalling until he changed his presentation strategy. Instead of leading with statistics about customer dissatisfaction, he began with a story that would transform how his colleagues viewed their work:

"Last Tuesday, Joan Mitchell tried to order her mother's heart medication through our website. After three failed attempts and forty minutes on hold with our service center, she missed her lunch break and had to drive thirty miles to the nearest pharmacy. Joan's story isn't unique—it's happening to our customers every day."

The impact was immediate and profound. Board members who had seemed indifferent to statistics suddenly became engaged, leaning forward in their chairs, asking questions about Joan's experience. Ryan had discovered what master persuaders have always known: stories create emotional investment in solutions in a way that data alone never can.

Following this initial success, Ryan developed a systematic approach to collecting and sharing customer experiences. He didn't just gather complaints—he sought out stories that illuminated both problems and possibilities. "I learned to look for stories that did three things," he explained during our session. "They had to be specific enough to feel real, universal enough to be relatable, and hopeful enough to suggest a solution."

His story collection process became increasingly sophisticated. He worked with customer service representatives to identify particularly meaningful interactions. He looked for customers who, despite frustrations, remained loyal because they believed in the company's potential. These stories of customer faith in the face of difficulties proved especially powerful in motivating change.

Ryan also discovered the importance of following up his stories with clear, achievable solutions. After sharing Joan's experience, he outlined specific changes that could have prevented her situation—an improved website interface, a callback system for long hold times, and partnerships with local pharmacies for emergency prescriptions. This combination of emotional impact and practical solutions proved irresistible. "Stories open hearts," he observed, "but they also open minds to new possibilities."

Secret #54: Appeal to Logic and Emotion

Diana's proposal for a major IT infrastructure upgrade gained unexpected traction when she learned to balance data with emotional appeal. Her presentation began with what she called the "foundation of facts," a detailed cost analysis of the current system, efficiency metrics, and ROI projections. But unlike her previous attempts, she didn't stop there.

Understanding that numbers alone rarely inspire action, Diana wove in the human impact of the current system's limitations. She shared stories of employees staying late because of slow system responses, of team collaborations disrupted by technical failures, and of innovative ideas abandoned because the infrastructure couldn't support them.

She painted vivid pictures of how improved systems would transform daily work life. "Imagine arriving at your desk and having immediate access to everything you need," she would say. "No more watching the spinning wheel, no more apologizing to clients for delays, no more losing work because of system crashes." These tangible benefits resonated with everyone who had ever felt frustrated by technical limitations.

Finally, she tied everything together with a clear vision forward. Her implementation timeline wasn't just a series of technical milestones—it was a story of transformation told through concrete, achievable steps. She shared personal stories of team members who were excited about the project's potential, making the benefits feel immediate and real.

"The data justified the investment," Diana noted, "but the human stories inspired the commitment." When an executive later asked why this proposal succeeded where previous attempts had failed, she explained, "Before, I was selling a system upgrade. This time, I was sharing a vision of a better workplace."

Secret #55: Turn Objections into Opportunities

When Carlos faced significant pushback to his team restructuring proposal, his instinct was to minimize objections. Instead, he tried something counterintuitive: he invited them. "I began each presentation by asking what concerns people had," he explained. "By addressing fears upfront, I transformed skeptics into collaborators."

His approach to handling objections became a masterclass in active listening. During meetings, he would take detailed notes, not just of what people said but of the emotions behind their words. When someone raised a concern about the proposed changes affecting team dynamics, Carlos didn't just record the objection—he noted the underlying worry about disrupting successful working relationships.

This deep listening approach allowed him to understand the root causes of resistance. Through careful questioning and genuine curiosity, he often discovered that apparent opposition to his proposals actually stemmed from unrelated concerns that could be addressed separately.

Secret #56: Create a Sense of Collaboration

Lauren's success in gaining buy-in for a controversial marketing strategy came from transforming her presentations into conversations. She developed what she calls "collaborative checkpoints," strategic moments throughout her proposals where she would pause to actively seek input and incorporate feedback.

"I stopped thinking of persuasion as a performance and started seeing it as a partnership. " This shift in mindset transformed her entire approach. Instead of presenting a fully formed plan, she would share the framework of her ideas and invite others to help shape the details. Each presentation became an opportunity for co-creation rather than mere approval-seeking.

During one particularly crucial presentation about rebranding, Lauren masterfully demonstrated this approach. After outlining each major change, she would pause and ask, "How could we make this work in your department?" These weren't perfunctory questions—she allocated significant time for discussion and kept detailed notes of every suggestion.

The resulting discussions not only improved her initial proposals but also created a sense of shared ownership that proved invaluable during implementation. Team members who might have resisted change became advocates because they saw their own ideas reflected in the final plan. Lauren discovered that people who participate in shaping a solution are naturally more invested in its success.

She made a habit of acknowledging contributions publicly and showing how each person's input improved the final outcome. During follow-up meetings, she would specifically reference suggestions and their positive impact: "Wendy's idea about phasing the rollout by department has already helped us identify and address potential issues early."

"The most powerful moment," Lauren recalled, "was when I heard a department head describing 'our new strategy' to his team. That's when I knew we'd succeeded—when it stopped being my proposal and became our shared vision."

Secret #57: Use a Call to Action

Jimmy learned that the end of a persuasive presentation is just the beginning of the journey. His successful campaign for departmental reorganization succeeded because he always ended with clear, actionable next steps. But more than that, he discovered the art of creating momentum through carefully crafted calls to action.

The key, Jimmy found, was making each request both specific and achievable. Rather than ending with vague suggestions like "let's improve communication," he would propose concrete actions: "Starting next week, we'll have fifteen-minute daily stand-ups at 9 a.m. to share progress and identify blockers." Each task had measurable outcomes that could be tracked and celebrated.

Yet he was careful not to overwhelm; he learned to start with small, manageable steps that built upon existing processes. "I used to end presentations with big, inspiring visions," Jimmy shared. "But I discovered that inspiration without direction quickly fades. Now I make sure everyone leaves knowing exactly what their first step should be."

A breakthrough came when Jimmy started treating his calls to action as bridges between vision and reality. He would carefully craft each request to build upon the previous one, creating a clear path from the current state to the desired outcome. This approach not only made change feel more manageable but also helped maintain enthusiasm throughout the implementation process.

Secret #58: Follow Up with Gratitude

Helen's ability to maintain momentum after initial agreement came from her understanding that gratitude isn't just polite—it's strategic. "A well-crafted thank-you can be as powerful as the initial persuasion," she explained. Her approach to follow-up transformed routine acknowledgments into opportunities for deepening commitment and building lasting relationships.

She developed a systematic approach that began with immediate appreciation. Within 24 hours of any agreement, she would send personalized thank-you notes that went beyond generic expressions of gratitude. Each note specifically acknowledged individual contributions and insights, showing that she had truly valued and remembered each person's input.

But Helen's approach to gratitude extended far beyond initial thanks. She understood that maintaining enthusiasm required regular progress updates that celebrated both small wins and major milestones. These weren't just status reports—they were carefully crafted narratives that connected current progress back to the original vision, reinforcing the wisdom of the initial decision.

"People often focus so much on getting to 'yes' that they forget about the journey after," Helen observed. "But that's where real relationships are built." She found that thoughtful follow-up did more than keep projects on track—it laid the ground-work for future collaboration and built her reputation as someone who valued not just results but relationships.

Perhaps most importantly, Helen learned to tailor her follow-up to each situation and relationship. A major strategic initiative might warrant formal progress reports and team celebra-tions, while a smaller project might need brief but regular check-ins. The key was maintaining connection and showing consistent appreciation for others' investment in shared success.

Moving Forward: Making Persuasion Personal

As we conclude this exploration of persuasion, remember that authentic influence isn't about techniques or tactics—it's about creating genuine connections and shared understand-ing. Start by building credibility through small, demonstrable successes. Take time to understand others' perspectives deeply before attempting to change their minds.

Use stories to create emotional investment in your ideas, but always balance narrative impact with practical solutions. Remember that resistance often masks valuable insights. Welcome objections as opportunities to strengthen both your proposals and your relationships.

Most importantly, view persuasion not as a single event but as an ongoing journey of collaboration and growth. When you focus on building shared visions rather than winning arguments, you create lasting change that benefits everyone involved.

In our next chapter, we'll explore how to apply these principles of influence in specific challenging situations, from navigating organizational change to building support for innovative ideas. The foundations you've learned here will serve as building blocks for even more sophisticated approaches to creating positive change.

Key Takeaways

- Trust and credibility must precede persuasion attempts.
- Understanding others' perspectives is crucial for effective influence.
- Stories create emotional connections that statistics alone cannot.
- Balance logical and emotional appeals for maximum impact.
- Address objections openly to build trust.
- Collaboration transforms resistance into partnership.
- Clear calls to action maintain momentum.

- Gratitude reinforces commitment and builds relationships.

Action Steps

1. Identify three ways to build credibility in your current role.
2. Practice perspective-taking interviews with colleagues.
3. Collect stories that illustrate your key messages.
4. Create a balanced presentation combining logic and emotion.
5. List common objections and prepare thoughtful responses.
6. Design collaborative checkpoints for your next proposal.
7. Develop clear, specific calls to action.
8. Create a systematic follow-up protocol.

Chapter 8
How to Leave a Conversation with Lasting Impressions

The hotel ballroom buzzed with post-conference energy as hundreds of attendees gathered their belongings, ready to head home. Yet a small group remained, clustered around Samantha, eagerly exchanging contact information and making plans for future collaborations. As a first-time speaker at this annual industry event, Samantha had somehow turned a fifteen-minute presentation into what promised to be years of meaningful professional relationships.

Later, when I asked her secret, she smiled. "I learned that every conversation—whether it's a formal presentation or a casual chat—is an opportunity to create a lasting connection. But it's not about being memorable for its own sake. It's about making others feel valued, understood, and inspired."

What made Samantha's approach so effective wasn't just what she said during her presentation but how she engaged with people before and after. She arrived early, connecting with attendees individually and learning their names and interests. During her talk, she wove these personal connections into her message, making each person feel seen and included. Afterward, she remembered specific details from earlier conversations, creating a sense of continuity that made people feel uniquely valued.

The Psychology of Lasting Impressions

Understanding how memories form and endure is fascinating, but it's also essential for anyone who wants to create meaningful connections. After years of studying human interaction patterns, I've discovered that the science of memory offers profound insights into the art of lasting impressions.

Recent neuroscience research has revealed that memory formation is far more selective than we once believed. Our brains don't passively record experiences like a video camera; instead, they actively choose what to remember based on emotional significance, novelty, and personal relevance. This selectivity explains why we might forget dozens of routine interactions but vividly remember one meaningful conversation years later.

What's particularly interesting is how our brains tag specific interactions as "important" while discarding others. Emotional engagement plays a crucial role—conversations that make us feel valued, understood, or inspired are far more likely to be encoded into long-term memory. This is why genuine connection often leaves a more lasting impression than a polished performance.

Our brains process thousands of interactions every day, yet only a select few leave a lasting mark. What makes certain conversations memorable while others fade into the background? The answer lies in understanding both the science of memory formation and the art of human connection. It's about learning to create what psychologists call "peak-end experiences," interactions that combine memorable high points with strong conclusions.

Secret #59: People Remember the First and Last Impressions

Marcus, a neuroscience researcher turned executive coach, transformed his approach to business relationships when he understood how human memory actually works. "Our brains aren't like video recorders, capturing everything equally," he explained during one of our sessions. "They're more like highlight reels, focusing intensely on beginnings and endings."

This cognitive science insight, known as the primacy and recency effect, revolutionized Marcus's approach to every interaction. Through his research and practical experience, he discovered that people might forget the middle of a conversation, but they almost always remember how it began and ended. This led him to develop what he calls "memory bookends," intentionally crafted openings and closings that make interactions memorable.

During a crucial client meeting, Marcus put this knowledge into practice in a way that would transform not just that meeting but his entire approach to business relationships. He began with a surprising observation about the client's office artwork, creating an immediate personal connection. "I noticed you have a Rothko print," he said. "It reminds me of how complex ideas can be expressed through seemingly simple forms—much like what we're trying to achieve with this project." This opening not only demonstrated his attentiveness but created a metaphor he could return to throughout the conversation.

Throughout the meeting, Marcus made subtle callbacks to this initial observation, weaving a thread of continuity. He referred back to the artwork when discussing project challenges: "Like the layers in that Rothko piece, we need to build this solution step by step." When wrapping up, he connected his final points to that first moment: "Just as that artwork creates impact through careful composition, our strategy will succeed through thoughtful integration of each element."

The client later described this meeting as "uniquely memorable" and "unlike any other consultation." When I asked Marcus about this approach, he explained that it's not just about creating clever bookends—it's about understanding how human memory works and using that knowledge to create meaningful connections.

"The key," Marcus shared, "is making those opening and closing moments authentic and relevant. It's not about memorizing scripts or forcing connections. It's about being genuinely present and finding natural ways to create memorable moments that reinforce your message."

After years of applying this science-based approach, Marcus developed several principles for creating memorable interactions. Before any important conversation, he would take a moment to consider what impression he wanted to leave. He learned to start with something specific and personal that could serve as a reference point throughout the discussion. Throughout each conversation, he would make thoughtful callbacks to earlier points, creating a sense of continuity and connection.

The science behind Marcus's approach is fascinating. Research has shown that our brains are particularly attuned to patterns and connections (Barkman, 2021). When we create thematic links throughout a conversation—like Marcus's art metaphor —we're actually helping our listeners' brains organize and retain information more effectively. These conversational threads become like mental handrails, giving people something familiar to grasp as they process new information.

The impact of this approach extended beyond individual meetings. Marcus found that clients and colleagues were more likely to implement his suggestions and seek his advice on future projects. "When you understand how memory works," he noted, "you can create experiences that don't just end when the conversation does—they continue to influence and inspire long after."

Secret #60: Balance Confidence With Humility

Jessica's journey from respected manager to beloved leader began when she learned this delicate balance. "I used to think confidence meant having all the answers," she shared during one of our coaching sessions. "Now I know it means being secure enough to admit what you don't know."

During a particularly challenging project review, Jessica demonstrated this balance perfectly. She presented her team's achievements with quiet assurance but readily acknowledged areas where they needed input from others. When a junior team member suggested an improvement to her proposal, she didn't just accept the feedback—she enthusiastically credited him for elevating the entire project.

"The real breakthrough came when I stopped trying to impress people and started trying to elevate them," Jessica explained. She developed a practice of what she calls "confident humility," which transformed her leadership style and her relationships with colleagues. This approach wasn't about diminishing her own expertise—it was about creating space for others to shine while maintaining her professional authority.

Jessica's approach to confident humility reflects a growing understanding in leadership psychology about the power of vulnerable authority. Studies have shown that leaders who can acknowledge their limitations while maintaining clear expertise actually build stronger trust than those who project infallibility. This balance creates what psychologists call "psychological safety"—an environment where others feel safe to contribute and take risks.

Secret #61: Infuse Conversations With Purpose

David's reputation for transformative conversations grew from his understanding that every interaction needs a clear purpose. As head of professional development at a global consulting firm, he turned routine check-ins into opportunities for growth and inspiration.

"Before any conversation, I ask myself three questions," David shared. "*What do I want the other person to feel? What do I want them to know? What do I want them to be inspired to do?*" This simple practice transformed his interactions from forgettable exchanges into meaningful moments of connection.

He demonstrated this approach during a seemingly routine performance review with a team member. Instead of just discussing metrics and goals, David created space for deeper exploration. "I sense you have bigger dreams than your current role allows," he observed. "Tell me about the impact you'd like to have in the next few years." This purposeful shift turned a standard review into a pivotal career moment for his colleague.

Through careful preparation and intentional questioning, David discovered that every conversation, no matter how routine it might seem, held the potential for transformation. He developed what he called his "purpose map," a mental framework for ensuring that each interaction served both immediate objectives and longer-term development goals.

David's focus on purposeful conversation aligns with recent findings in cognitive psychology about how our brains process and retain information. When we enter an interaction with clear intentions, we activate neural networks that help us filter and organize information more effectively. This preparation literally changes how our brains engage with the conversation, making it more likely that both parties will find the interaction meaningful and memorable.

Secret #62: Be a Source of Inspiration

Rachel discovered that being inspirational isn't about grand gestures or motivational speeches—it's about helping others see possibilities they hadn't considered before. As a mentor to young professionals, she developed what she calls "possibility conversations."

During one memorable interaction with a discouraged junior analyst, Rachel didn't just offer comfort—she helped him reframe his challenges as opportunities. "I notice you have a particular talent for simplifying complex data," she observed. "Have you considered how that skill might be valuable in client communications?"

This ability to spot and articulate others' unique strengths became Rachel's signature. She found that people remembered her not for what she said about herself but for how she helped them see their own potential. She developed a keen eye for identifying hidden talents and creating opportunities for people to showcase them.

Secret #63: Foster a Sense of Belonging

When Alex took over leadership of a fragmented global team, he realized that technical expertise alone wouldn't create the cohesion they needed. His breakthrough came from understanding that lasting impressions are built on emotional connections.

During virtual team meetings, Alex started dedicating the first few minutes to what he called "connection moments." Team members would share not just project updates but personal victories, challenges, or cultural celebrations. These moments transformed their interactions from transactional to deeply personal.

"In a digital world, belonging doesn't happen automatically," Alex noted. "We have to create it intentionally." He made a practice of recognizing individual contributions while tying them back to the team's shared mission, helping each person see their unique place in the larger story.

This approach proved particularly powerful during challenging projects. When team members felt personally connected to each other and the mission, they showed greater resilience and creativity in solving problems. Alex discovered that strong emotional bonds created a foundation for exceptional performance.

Secret #64: End Every Interaction with Gratitude

Maria transformed her consulting practice when she learned that gratitude isn't just a polite gesture—it's a powerful tool for creating lasting connections. She developed a practice of ending every client meeting by expressing specific, genuine appreciation for something she had learned or gained from the interaction.

"It's not about generic thank-yous," Maria explained. "It's about helping people understand the unique value they bring." She would often follow up conversations with handwritten notes highlighting specific insights or contributions that had impacted her thinking.

The power of Maria's approach lie in its specificity and authenticity. Rather than offering blanket appreciation, she would point to particular moments or ideas that had made a difference. This attention to detail showed people that they had been truly heard and valued.

Secret #65: Build Bridges to the Future

Stephen's ability to turn single conversations into long-term relationships came from his understanding that every ending should point toward a beginning. As a business development executive, he transformed standard networking events into launching pads for meaningful collaboration.

Rather than ending conversations with vague "let's stay in touch" statements, Stephen would create specific connection points. "I'd love to learn more about your approach to sustainability," he might say. "Could we schedule a virtual coffee next week to dive deeper into that topic?"

His follow-through was equally intentional. He maintained what he called a "connection map," a system for tracking conversation threads and shared interests that he could reference in future interactions. This attention to detail made his follow-ups feel natural and personally relevant rather than forced or generic.

Creating Your Legacy of Connection

As we conclude this exploration of lasting impressions, remember that memorable interactions aren't about performance or technique—they're about creating genuine value and connection. Start by understanding how memory works and crafting thoughtful openings and closings that resonate with your audience.

Practice balancing confidence with humility and remember that true authority comes from elevating others while maintaining your own expertise. Infuse every conversation with a clear purpose, looking for opportunities to inspire and encourage those around you.

Most importantly, remember that lasting impressions are built on emotional connections. Foster belonging, express genuine gratitude, and always build bridges to future interactions. When you approach each conversation as an opportunity to create value for others, you naturally create experiences that endure long after the moment has passed.

The journey to mastering lasting impressions is ongoing, but with these principles as your guide, you're well-equipped to create meaningful connections that stand the test of time. Remember, it's not about being memorable for its own sake— it's about making others feel valued, understood, and inspired to achieve their full potential.

Key Takeaways

- The beginning and end of interactions create the strongest memories.

- Balance confidence with humility to build authentic connections.
- Purpose-driven conversations create lasting impact.
- Inspiration comes from helping others see their potential.
- Creating a sense of belonging strengthens relationships.
- Genuine gratitude reinforces meaningful connections.
- Building future bridges turns conversations into relationships.

Action Steps

1. Practice crafting intentional openings and closings for important conversations.
2. Develop your own style of "confident humility."
3. Create purpose statements for significant interactions.
4. Build a collection of inspiring questions and observations.
5. Design "connection moments" for your team or group interactions.
6. Start a gratitude practice for professional relationships.
7. Develop a system for meaningful follow up.

Bonus: Seven Keys to Enhance Talking Mastery

Key 1: Setting Your Foundation

Activity 1: Know Yourself

Ask yourself these questions to assess your communication skills.

1. How do you define effective communication from your perspective?
2. Do you struggle to find the right words to express your thoughts and feelings?
3. Can you read people's body language?
4. Do you prefer communicating through text messages or in person?
5. Do you struggle with communicating complex emotions?
6. Do you struggle with understanding other people's points of view?

7. Do people often misunderstand you or find your words confusing?

8. Do you ask questions when you don't understand what the other person is saying, or do you let it go and stay silent?

9. Do people often ask you to elaborate on your words?

10. Do you actively listen when people talk to you, or do you zone out and get distracted?

11. How do you handle disagreements or conflicts during conversation?

12. How do you handle conversations with difficult individuals?

13. How do you convey your message to a large group of people?

14. What do you do when you and a coworker have different opinions about a project you are working on?

15. How do you communicate with your team at work?

16. Have you ever used the power of persuasion to change someone's mind?

17. Do you raise your voice when someone disagrees with you?

18. Are you a compassionate listener?

19. What makes you a good conversationalist?

20. What do you need to change to be a better conversationalist?

Reading your answers will help you evaluate your communication skills.

Activity 2: Setting SMART Goals

- **Specific:** Avoid general statements when setting goals, such as "I want to be a better conversationalist." You need to be more specific. For instance, do you need to work on your listening skills? Or do you need to be more articulate?

- Ask yourself these questions to help you determine your goals.
  - What do you need to accomplish?
  - How will achieving this goal impact your life?
  - What do you need to do to achieve your goal?

- **Measurable:** Your goals should be measurable, allowing you to track your progress. Simply, you need to determine how you will know when your goal is accomplished. This will help you stay motivated and focused on your conversational goals.
- **Achievable:** Goals should be realistic, attainable, and within your skills and abilities. Unrealistic goals are impossible to achieve and will cause disappointment and lower your self-esteem. Ask yourself if you have what it takes to achieve your goal and if it is achievable.
- **Relevant:** Your goal should align with your future aspirations. For instance, you may want to improve your conversational skills and become a better listener to communicate effectively with your coworkers and boss to advance your career.
  - Ask yourself these questions:
    - Is your goal worthwhile?
    - Is it the right time to work on achieving your goal?
    - Is it relevant to your needs?
    - Realistically, can you achieve your goal?

- **Time-Bound:** Goals should have a deadline to keep you focused and prevent daily tasks from distracting you. However, the deadline should be realistic to give you time to work on your conversational skills.
    - What can you do today to get closer to your goal?
    - What can you do in a week to achieve your goal?
    - What can you do in a month to achieve your goal?

Your Task

Practicing by writing down your initial thoughts and confidence levels in a journal. This will create a baseline for future reflection. You need to recognize where you stand. Honest self-assessment is the cornerstone of growth. Focus on identifying patterns in your communication—areas where you excel and those that need work. Setting clear and actionable goals ensures your progress is measurable and rewarding.

Key 2: Master Active Listening

Activity 1: Knowing the Importance of Reflective Listening

Reflective listening is a communication technique that involves asking questions, paraphrasing, or repeating the speaker's words to understand what they are trying to communicate to you. This prevents misunderstanding and makes the speaker feel heard and validated.

For instance, your friend complains that their boss ignores their ideas and doesn't take them seriously. You can respond by paraphrasing what they said and validating their emotions, "I am sure it's frustrating to feel overlooked at work, especially when you have many creative ideas."

- Acknowledge their feelings using phrases such as, "I sense that you are feeling angry" or "It sounds like you are upset."
- Validate them by showing that you understand what they are going through. For example, you could say, "I understand what you mean and would feel the same way if I were in this situation."
- Paraphrase their words by reflecting on the thoughts, emotions, ideas, or opinions they have shared. You can say, "If I understand correctly, you are saying it bothers you when your partner cancels plans without explaining why."
- Use the mirroring technique by repeating the last few words they said to show that you are paying attention to the conversation.

Example:
A: Traveling is a great experience. I had a great time backpacking through Europe.
B: Wow, you backpacked through Europe! What was that like?

- Summarize the main points of the conversation, especially when the speaker has shared certain concerns, to ensure you understand what they are saying. For instance, your boss says that the team didn't come up with any original ideas in the last few months, and the company is losing money. Respond by saying, "So you are saying that we need to be more creative and work harder to save our company."
- If you don't understand what the speaker is saying, ask for clarification or open-ended questions that start with "what," "how," or "why." These let the

speaker elaborate on their words and broaden the discussion. Avoid close-ended questions that can only be answered with "yes" or "no," which shortens the conversation.

- Be objective and avoid personal biases or making assumptions. This will create a safe space for the speaker to share their thoughts and emotions without feeling judged or attacked.
- Be empathetic and put yourself in their shoes before responding.
- Support and encourage them when they need it.

Practice reflective listening by paraphrasing what others say. You can try this skill with your partner, friends, or coworkers.

Activity 2: Things to remember to be an active listener

- Give the speaker your undivided attention and eliminate distractions by putting your phone in your pocket/bag, ignoring your inner dialogue, and refraining from daydreaming.
- Pay attention to their body language and facial expressions.
- Maintain eye contact.
- Ask open-ended questions like, "What do you think about that?" or "Can you tell me more about it?"
- Don't interrupt them, even if they struggle to find the words. Be patient and allow them to finish speaking before responding.
- Don't respond right away. Take a moment to reflect on what they said and organize your thoughts so that you can give an appropriate response.

- The HEAR Method: Hold your response (resist the urge to plan what you'll say next). Engage with body language (nod, maintain appropriate eye contact). Ask clarifying questions. Reflect key points back to the speaker.

Your Tasks

Choose a five-minute segment of your favorite podcast:

1. Close your eyes while listening.
2. Notice not just the words but the emotions behind them.
3. Try to catch subtle shifts in tone and pace.

Watch a 10-minute TED talk:

1. Take minimal notes.
2. Summarize the main points in three sentences.
3. Identify the speaker's core message.

Note improvements in comprehension and identify any challenges while you engage in any conversations.

Key 3: Strengthen Nonverbal Communication

Activity 1: Power Poses

You can use different power poses to boost your confidence before speaking.

- **The Mr. Clean:** Roll back your shoulders and cross your arms.

- **The Flying Superhero/The Victory Pose:** This is similar to Superman lifting his arms before taking flight. Make fists with both hands and lift your arms to make a "V" shape. This is a great pose to celebrate victory or good news. You can also practice this pose before a job interview. Imagine you get the job, and you celebrate yourself. This will give you confidence and self-assurance.
- **The Loomer:** This pose is perfect for public speaking. If you are sitting or standing behind a podium or a table, lean forward and place your hands on it.
- **The Peter Pan:** Stand straight with your legs wide apart, placing both hands on your hips. Hold your head high and plant your feet deeply on the ground.
- **The Wonder Woman:** Stand up straight, tilt your chin upward, and place your hands on your sides.

Activity 2: Do the Affirmations

Affirmations are positive phrases that you repeat every day to silence your inner critic and challenge negative thoughts. Repeat affirmations before speaking to raise your self-esteem.

- I believe in myself.
- I am enough.
- I am strong and powerful.
- I have the skills to achieve all my goals.
- I can overcome any challenges.
- I am a great conversationalist.
- People enjoy listening to my stories.
- I am smart, funny, and charismatic.
- My opinion is valuable.
- I have great ideas.

- I trust my intuition.
- I am proud of my achievements.
- I attract positive people into my life.
- I am constantly learning and growing.
- I am worthy of respect, love, and friendship.
- I am brave.
- My voice is powerful.
- I trust myself.
- I express myself with ease.

Activity 3: Practicing Eye Contact

- Start making eye contact before they start talking.
- Make eye contact 70% when listening and 50% when speaking.
- Maintain eye contact for five seconds, then look away slowly and glance to the sides for two or three seconds before resuming your gaze.
- If looking at someone's eyes makes you uncomfortable, look at other parts of their face, such as their mouth, chin, or nose.
- Instead of looking away, break your gaze by nodding or smiling when appropriate.

Your Tasks

Begin your day with Amy Cuddy's confidence-building poses:

1. Stand tall, hands on hips (Wonder Woman pose) for two minutes.
2. Raise arms in victory position for two minutes.
3. Notice how your energy shifts.
4. Journal about any changes in your confidence level.

Study these master communicators:

1. Michelle Obama: Watch for warmth and engagement.
2. Simon Sinek: Notice purposeful gestures.
3. Brené Brown: Observe authentic presence.

Choose one video above and:

1. Watch without sound for two minutes.
2. Mirror their movements.
3. Note which gestures feel natural.
4. Incorporate one new gesture into your repertoire.

Track Progress

- Which nonverbal habits have you discovered about yourself
- Which gestures felt most authentic to your style

Key 4: Develop Impromptu Speaking Skills

Impromptu speaking is thinking on your feet and speaking on the spot without preparation. However, the speaker should be familiar with the topic discussed and able to talk about it on the spur of the moment. For instance, you're reading a new book, and You are out with your partner's coworkers, and they start discussing the book. If you are uncomfortable speaking with people you have just met, you may struggle with organizing your thoughts and engaging in the conversation. However, a confident speaker will express their thoughts easily and provide their opinion about the book without hesitation.

This skill will benefit you in various areas of your life, such as job interviews, work meetings, debates, or friendly discussions.

Tips for Practicing Impromptu Speaking

- Practice active listening to grasp what the speaker is saying before responding.
- Take time to process the information the speaker is sharing with you.
- While impromptu speaking requires quick thinking, you should still take a moment to organize your thoughts and words and decide what you will contribute to the discussion.
- Discuss the topic like a narrative with a beginning, middle, and end. Introduce the topic, explain it, share your perspective, and suggest how to improve it.

Practice impromptu speaking on random topics for one minute. You can do this with someone you are comfortable with, such as a friend or family member.

Activity 1: The One-Minute Expert

Speaking about topics you know well, such as:

- a favorite book or movie
- a skill you've recently learned
- a place you love
- a problem you've solved

Activity 2: Power Phrases for Confidence

Replace hesitant language with power phrases:

- Instead of "I think maybe…" use "I believe…"
- Instead of "I'm not sure but…" use "In my experience…"
- Instead of "This might be wrong…" use "My perspective is…"

Your Tasks

1. Participate in a short debate or discussion.

2. Practice impromptu speaking on random topics for one minute. You can do this with someone you are comfortable with, such as a friend or family member.

3. Practice stating opinions confidently as follows:

- Choose three topics you care about.
- Write and deliver clear position statements.
- Record yourself and analyze your tone.
- Adjust for balance of confidence and openness.

4. Think about this:

- Moments when you felt most confident speaking
- Situations where you held back
- Specific phrases or tones that enhanced your message

Key 5: Achieve Clarity and Articulation

Activity 1: Practice Tongue Twisters

Perform tongue twisters and enunciation exercises.

- Betty bought butter, but the butter was bitter, so

Betty bought better butter to make the bitter butter better.

- If practice makes perfect and perfect needs practice, I'm perfectly practiced and practically perfect.
- Peter Piper picked a peck of pickled peppers. A peck of pickled peppers Peter Piper picked. If Peter Piper picked a peck of pickled peppers, Where's the peck of pickled peppers Peter Piper picked?
- I thought a thought. But the thought I thought wasn't the thought I thought I thought. If the thought I thought I thought had been the thought I thought, I wouldn't have thought I thought.
- She sells seashells by the seashore.
- If you must cross a course cross cow across a crowded cow crossing, cross the cross coarse cow across the crowded cow crossing carefully.
- Susie works in a shoeshine shop. Where she shines, she sits, and where she sits, she shines.
- Brisk, brave brigadiers brandished broad, bright blades, blunderbusses, and bludgeons—balancing them badly.
- How much wood would a woodchuck chuck if a woodchuck could chuck wood? He would chuck, he would, as much as he could, and chuck as much wood as a woodchuck would if a woodchuck could chuck wood.

Activity 2: Improve Your Enunciation

Enunciation is speaking clearly to appear powerful and confident. It focuses on pronunciation, voice volume, breathing, speech speed, and connecting words together.

- Stand up straight when practicing enunciation exercises. This makes speaking and pronunciation easier. You should also relax your shoulders and arms.
- Take a deep breath before you start.
- Open your mouth wide as if you are at the dentist.
- Speak slowly.
- Speak each word distinctly and clearly.
- Speak in a proper volume to make sure your audience can hear you. Avoid raising or straining your voice.
- Don't mumble, slur, rush, or stumble over your words.
- The tone of your voice, your pitch, and your breathing should be in balance.
- Watch yourself in the mirror while speaking, and pay attention to your tongue, teeth, jaw, and lips while you pronounce every word.
- Put a pencil between your teeth, read a book aloud, and speak every word clearly. In this exercise, you will depend on your tongue instead of your mouth, enhancing its flexibility.

Activity 3: Using The PREP Method

Choose any topic and practice your thoughts in the following steps:

1. Point (state your main idea).
2. Reason (support with evidence).
3. Example (illustrate with a story).
4. Point (reinforce your message).

Your Tasks

1. Explain a concept simply to a friend or ten-year-old kid.

2. Document to yourself:

- Instances where you simplified complex ideas successfully
- Moments when clarity was challenging
- Techniques that helped you communicate more effectively

Key 6: Spark Engaging Conversations

Activity 1: Create engaging questions

The F.O.R.D. technique, for example:

Family:

- "What family traditions do you cherish most?"
- "How has your family influenced your career choices?"

Occupation:

- "What inspired you to choose your current field?"
- "What's the most rewarding part of your work?"

Recreation:

- "What do you do to recharge after a busy week?"
- "What hobby would you love to master?"

Dreams:

- "What's one goal you're working toward right now?"
- "Where do you see yourself in five years?"

The Follow-Up Formula

After each response, use:

- "Tell me more about…"
- "What led you to…"
- "How did you feel when…"
- "What impact did that have on…"

The Connection Bridge

Practice linking topics naturally:

- Find common threads.
- Share related experiences.
- Ask comparative questions.
- Build on shared interests.

Activity 2: Shared Settings

Initiate and maintain a conversation in a shared setting. For instance, if you have a doctor's appointment, start a conversation with the person sitting next to you or invite your new coworker for coffee and get to know them better. This will help you gain confidence and build good relationships at your workplace.

Your Tasks

- Keep in mind your list of F.O.R.D. questions and follow-ups that you created.
- Think about your examples of connection bridges.
- Reflections on your role-playing practice and shared-setting conversations.

Key 7: Integration and Mastery

Activity: Reflect and Plan

Take a moment at the end of your day to reflect:

- Most engaging conversations of the day
- Questions that sparked meaningful responses
- Moments where you could have dug deeper
- Successful topic transitions

Identify which of your new conversational skills improved and which require more work and training. As you should:

- Notice patterns in your growth.
- Celebrate your progress.
- Set intentions for continued development.

Your Task

After reviewing your strengths and weaknesses, write a self-assessment reflecting on your progress and areas for continued growth. Be proud of what you have accomplished so far. Create a plan to keep working on your conversation skills and commit to it.

Your Journey Forward

As we conclude these seven keys above, remember that mastery isn't a destination—it's an ongoing process of growth and refinement. Keep 65 simple secrets here with you, stay curious about your communication patterns, and, most importantly, maintain compassion for yourself as you continue to grow. Every conversation is an opportunity to practice, learn, and connect more deeply with others.

Remember:

- Progress comes from consistent practice.
- Authenticity matters more than perfection.
- Small improvements compound over time.
- Connection is the ultimate goal.

Conclusion

Last week, I received an email that brought tears to my eyes. It was from Thomas, a former client who had struggled with severe social anxiety. "Remember how I used to hide in my office during team lunches?" he wrote. "Yesterday, I gave the keynote speech at our industry conference. As I stood at the podium, looking out at hundreds of faces, I felt something I never expected—joy."

Thomas's journey from hiding to speaking wasn't just about overcoming anxiety—it was about discovering his authentic voice and learning to share it with the world. His transformation reminds us that the greatest barriers to communication often aren't external obstacles but internal beliefs about who we are and what we're capable of becoming.

Thomas's story isn't unique. Throughout this book, we've shared the journeys of many others—Sarah, who transformed from avoiding client calls to leading sales meetings; Maya, who went from dreading networking events to organizing them; James, who evolved from the quiet engineer to his company's most effective communicator. Their successes weren't about becoming different people—they were about becoming more fully themselves while developing the skills to share that authenticity with others.

Consider Sarah's path. Although her technical expertise has always been exceptional, she used to view client calls as necessary evils to endure. Through practicing the principles we've discussed, she discovered that her detailed understanding of complex systems actually made her an excellent communicator—once she learned to translate that knowledge into stories and metaphors that resonated with others. Today, clients specifically request her for challenging projects, not just for her technical skills but also for her ability to build trust and understanding.

Maya's transformation was equally profound. She once saw networking events as battlegrounds of forced small talk and superficial connections. By applying the principles of authentic engagement we've explored, she realized that these events could be opportunities for genuine connection and mutual growth. Now, she creates spaces where others who share her former hesitation can find their own path to meaningful professional relationships.

James's evolution from quiet engineer to effective communicator particularly resonates with many readers. He didn't need to become louder or more extroverted—instead, he learned to leverage his natural thoughtfulness and precision in ways that enhanced his communication. Once hidden behind silence, his careful listening skills became one of his greatest strengths in building team collaboration.

As we conclude our journey together, I want to share what I consider the most profound truth I've discovered in my years of studying human connection: The ability to talk to anyone isn't about mastering a set of techniques—it's about mastering yourself. It's about finding your authentic voice, understanding your unique strengths, and learning to share these gifts with others in ways that create meaningful connections.

Throughout this book, we have explored 65 secrets of effective communication. We have delved into the art of active listening, the power of nonverbal cues, the impact of storytelling, and the importance of emotional intelligence. We have also practiced specific techniques, from power posing to the FORD method, from the triangle technique of eye contact to the PREP framework for clear communication.

But these aren't just techniques to be memorized—they're tools for authentic expression. Think of them as instruments in an orchestra. Just as a musician must first master individual instruments before creating a symphony, you've learned individual communication skills that you can now combine into your unique style of connection. The goal isn't to play someone else's music but to create your own harmonious way of engaging with the world.

The journey doesn't end here. In fact, this is where it truly begins. Every conversation is an opportunity to practice, refine, and grow. Every interaction is a chance to deepen your understanding of yourself and others. The skills you've learned aren't meant to be perfect—they're meant to be practiced.

Think of each interaction as a small experiment in connection. Some will go exactly as you hope, and others might feel awkward or uncertain. Both outcomes are valuable—success builds confidence, while challenges provide opportunities for growth and learning. The key is to maintain curiosity about both yourself and others throughout the process.

Remember these essential truths as you move forward:

- Your voice matters. The world needs your unique perspective, experiences, and insights. No one else can contribute quite what you can to a conversation or relationship. Your authenticity is your greatest asset.
- Connection is a two-way street. The best conversations aren't performances—they're exchanges. When you focus on creating value for others and remaining genuinely curious about their perspectives, a meaningful connection naturally follows.
- Growth is ongoing. Even the most skilled communicators continue to learn and evolve. Every person you meet, every conversation you have offers new insights and opportunities for refinement of your skills.
- Authenticity trumps perfection. People connect with real humans, not polished performances. Your willingness to be genuine, even when it means showing vulnerability, creates stronger bonds than any perfectly executed technique.
- Every interaction is an opportunity. Small moments can lead to meaningful connections. A simple exchange at a coffee shop, a brief conversation with a colleague, or a quick chat with a neighbor—all can become stepping stones to deeper relationships.

As you move forward on your communication journey, I encourage you to:

- **Start Small**: Begin with one technique at a time. Master it in low-stakes situations before adding complexity. Perhaps practice active listening during casual conversations with friends before applying it in high-pressure professional situations.

- **Stay Curious**: Approach each conversation as an opportunity to learn something new about others and yourself. What patterns do you notice in your interactions? What techniques feel most natural to you? What situations still challenge you?
- **Embrace Imperfection**: Remember that meaningful connections come from authentic sharing, not flawless execution. Your willingness to be real, to sometimes stumble, to learn and grow, makes you more relatable and trustworthy.
- **Celebrate Progress**: Notice and acknowledge your growth, no matter how small it might seem. Did you maintain eye contact more comfortably? Did you ask more engaging questions? Did you feel more at ease in a typically stressful situation? These are all wins worth celebrating.
- **Keep Practicing**: Make communication practice a daily habit, just like any other important skill. Set small, achievable goals for each day or week. Maybe it's initiating one new conversation, trying one new technique, or pushing slightly beyond your comfort zone in a safe situation.

Most importantly, remember that your journey to becoming a more effective communicator isn't about changing who you are—it's about becoming more fully yourself and sharing that self more effectively with the world.

Let me share one final story. During the break at a recent workshop, a participant named Rachel approached me. "I always thought some people were just born good communicators," she said. Now I understand that it's not about being born with it—it's about building it, one conversation at a time."

Rachel's insight captures the essence of what I hope you'll take from this book. The ability to talk to anyone isn't a gift bestowed upon a lucky few—it's a skill that anyone can develop with practice, patience, and persistence.

As you close this book and step back into your world, remember that every conversation is an opportunity to practice these skills, every interaction a chance to deepen your understanding, and every connection an opportunity to grow. The techniques and strategies we've explored are now yours to use, adapt, and make your own.

Your journey to becoming a more effective communicator doesn't end here—in many ways, it's just beginning. Take these tools, make them your own, and watch as your ability to connect with others transforms both your professional and personal life.

Remember Thomas, Sarah, Maya, James, and all the others whose stories we've shared. They started exactly where you are now. Their success wasn't about natural talent or lucky breaks —it was about consistent practice, genuine effort, and the courage to keep growing.

Now it's your turn. The world is waiting to hear your voice, benefit from your insights, and connect with your authentic self. Take that first step, start that conversation, make that connection. Your next meaningful interaction could be the beginning of something extraordinary.

Thank You!

I truly appreciate you for choosing the book out of so many books available! It means a lot that you not only picked it up but also made it all the way to the end. Thank you for your time, trust, and commitment to improving your communication skills.

Before you go, I have a small favor to ask—if you found value in this book, would you consider leaving a review on the platform? The book is on my profile page in the link below. Your feedback is incredibly important and helps independent authors like me continue creating content that empowers readers like you. Your thoughts, insights, and experiences could also inspire someone else to start their own journey toward better conversations and stronger connections. I'd love to hear from you!

Thank you again for your support—it truly means the world to me!

View my profile page at:

https://www.amazon.com/author/parkerlawson1

References

Aknin, L. B., Dunn, E. W., Proulx, J., Lok, I., & Norton, M. I. (2020). Does spending money on others promote happiness? A registered replication report. *Journal of Personality and Social Psychology, 119*(2), 15–26. https://doi.org/10.1037/pspa0000191

Barkman, R. (2021, May 19). Why the human brain is so good at detecting patterns. *Psychology Today.* https://www.psychologytoday.com/us/blog/singular-perspective/202105/why-the-human-brain-is-so-good-detecting-patterns

Carney, D. R., Cuddy, A. J. C., & Yap, A. J. (2010). Power posing: Brief nonverbal displays affect neuroendocrine levels and risk tolerance. *Psychological Science, 21*(10), 1363–1368. https://doi.org/10.1177/0956797610383437

Coupland, J. (2000). *Small talk.* Longman.

Ybarra, O., Winkielman, P., Yeh, I., Burnstein, E., & Kavanagh, L. (2010). Friends (and sometimes enemies) with cognitive benefits. *Social Psychological and Personality Science, 2*(3), 253–261. https://doi.org/10.1177/1948550610386808

Bell, S. (2024). *SMART goals.* Mind Tools. https://www.mindtools.com/a4wol18/smart-goals

Boogaard, K. (2023, December 26). How to write SMART goals. *Atlassian.* https://www.atlassian.com/blog/productivity/how-to-write-smart-goals

Communication interview questions & answers. (2024, January 23). *Clevry.* https://www.clevry.com/en/resources/competency-based-interview-questions/communication-interview-questions-answers/

Corporate Class Inc. (2021, December 14). *Assess your own interpersonal communication skills.* Corporate Class Inc. https://www.corporateclassinc.com/how-to-assess-your-own-interpersonal-communication-skills/

Herrity, J. (2024, April 9). How to write SMART goals (with examples). *Indeed.* https://www.indeed.com/career-advice/career-development/how-to-write-smart-goals

Carter, A. (2023, November 23). Reflective listening: A definitive guide. *Master Public Speaking & Presentation Skills | CJM Training.* https://colinjames-method.com/what-is-reflective-listening/

Cuncic, A. (2024, February 12). 7 active listening techniques for better communication. *Verywell Mind.* https://www.verywellmind.com/what-is-active-listening-3024343

Tennant, K., Butler, T. J. T., & Long, A. (2023). Active listening. *StatPearls*. https://www.ncbi.nlm.nih.gov/books/NBK442015/

Segal, J. (2024, September 25). *Body language and nonverbal communication.* HelpGuide. https://www.helpguide.org/relationships/communication/nonverbal-communication

Van Edwards, V. (2015, August 7). *Mirroring body language: 4 steps to successfully mirror.* Science of People. https://www.scienceofpeople.com/mirroring/

Barnard, D. (2021, March 2). How to give an impromptu speech, with examples. *VirtualSpeech*. https://virtualspeech.com/blog/how-to-give-an-impromptu-speech

How to power pose like a pro. (2020). *Headspace*. https://www.headspace.com/articles/how-to-power-pose-like-a-pro

Menezes, L. (2023, June 14). 30 positive affirmations for confidence. *UWS London*. https://www.uwslondon.ac.uk/mental-health/positive-affirmations-for-confidence/

Miles, M. (2023, May 2). Power poses: 6 examples to unleash your inner confidence. *BetterUp*. https://www.betterup.com/blog/power-poses

Oko-Odoi, K. (2023, October 25). The art of speaking on the fly: 6 strategies for impromptu speech. *Copper*. https://www.copper.com/resources/the-art-of-speaking-on-the-fly-6-strategies-for-impromptu-speech

75 tongue twisters in English. (n.d.). *BYJUS*. https://byjus.com/english/tongue-twisters/

Alex. (2019). 50 tongue twisters to improve pronunciation in English. *EngVid*. https://www.engvid.com/english-resource/50-tongue-twisters-improve-pronunciation/

Hishon, K. (n.d.). 6 tips to improve enunciation. *Theatrefolk*. https://www.theatrefolk.com/blog/6-tips-to-improve-enunciation

Simpson, E. (2024, November 15). How to enunciate better in English: 8 expert tips. *BoldVoice*. https:// www.boldvoice.com /blog /how-to-enunciate-better #id2

Thoman, L. (2023, November 3). How to enunciate better. *Backstage*. https://www.backstage.com/magazine/article/how-to-enunciate-better-76619/